GOLD

GOLD

How Gretzky's Men Ended
Canada's 50-Year
Olympic Hockey Drought

Tim Wharnsby

TRIUMPH
BOOKS

Library of Congress Cataloging-in-Publication Data available upon request.

This book is available in quantity at special discounts for your group or organization. For further information, contact:

Triumph Books LLC
814 North Franklin Street
Chicago, Illinois 60610
(312) 337-0747
www.triumphbooks.com

Printed in U.S.A.
ISBN: 978-1-62937-924-1
Photos by Fred Lum courtesy of the *Globe and Mail* unless otherwise specified
Design by Patricia Frey

To my cherished love, Kathy
My late parents; brother, David; sisters, Liz and Cathy
And to the dearly missed Canadian treasure Christie Blatchford

CONTENTS

FOREWORD

On my draft day in Quebec City in 1993, I was selected second by the Hartford Whalers after the Ottawa Senators chose my Canadian world junior teammate Alexandre Daigle first overall. Alex told reporters that day, "I'm glad I got drafted first, because no one remembers No. 2."

For that remark, my stick accidentally ran up and down the back of his legs a few times when the Whalers met the Senators. I finished first enough in my career to know the wonderful feeling of winning, including my first of two Olympic gold medals, in 2002.

A frequent question I'm asked is where my Olympic gold in Salt Lake City ranks compared to the other successes—a Stanley Cup win, a rare double-win of the Norris and Hart Trophies, a world championship title, and a world junior title. My response is always that each accomplishment is exceptional, and each feat plays an essential part in my Hockey Hall of Fame career.

I'm proud to be a member of the Triple Gold Club. I became the 19th member of the prestigious group when the Anaheim Ducks won the Stanley Cup in early June 2007 to go along with my 1997 World Championship and Olympic gold in 2002. I won another Olympic gold medal in 2010.

Suiting up for Canada in Salt Lake City at the 2002 Winter Olympics was extra special for so many reasons. While it's cool to be singled out with individual honours like the Norris Trophy and Hart Trophy in 2000, team championships are what the sport of hockey is all about.

To be part of the 2002 Canadian Olympic team was exceptional because we finally brought the gold medal back to Canada after 50 long years. We were able to overcome the heartbreak of the shootout loss to the Czech Republic four years earlier.

The 2002 team was such a star-studded group. How many Hall of Famers? Fourteen, and that number easily could expand with outstanding players like Curtis Joseph, Theo Fleury, Adam Foote, and others who have been overlooked.

When I glance up and down the Canadian roster, there are so many memories and connections that come to mind. Al MacInnis was a mentor and longtime teammate with the St. Louis Blues. My first championship wearing the Canadian maple leaf happened a few days into the New Year in 1993 at the World Junior Championship in Gavle, Sweden. We had a young team. Five of us went first (Alexandre Daigle), second (me), third (Chris Gratton), fourth (Paul Kariya), and fifth (Rob Niedermayer) in the NHL draft six months later. Paul, of course, was a teammate in Salt Lake City.

How could anyone predict my pass off the rush to Mario Lemieux in the slot that he let go through his legs to Paul in the gold medal final would wind up being such an important goal in the 2002 tournament?

I was traded for two of my 2002 teammates. In July 1995, I went from Hartford to St. Louis in exchange for Brendan Shanahan. In July 2005, I moved from St. Louis to Edmonton in a multi-player deal that sent Eric Brewer the other way.

I even played with Wayne Gretzky, our executive director and leader in 2002, for 18 regular season games and 13 more in the playoffs in his brief stop in St. Louis to finish the 1995–96 season. We also were teammates for Canada in the 1996 World Cup of Hockey and 1998 Olympics.

I played with Rob Blake, Jarome Iginla, and Owen Nolan when we captured gold at the 1997 World Championship in Helsinki, Finland. I performed with many of these guys with Canada in the 1996 World Cup of Hockey: Blake, Martin Brodeur, Theo Fleury, Foote, Joseph, Jovanovski, Eric Lindros, Scott Niedermayer, Joe Sakic, Shanahan, and Steve Yzerman.

Yzerman broke our hearts in St. Louis with that blast to give the Red Wings the win in double overtime of Game 7 in the second round in 1996. Belfour was at his best for Dallas to beat us three times in overtime in the second round in 1999.

I played in four Olympic Games with Martin Brodeur, the only two players to turn the trick. I played with Ryan Smyth in Edmonton, Scott Niedermayer in Anaheim, and Simon Gagne in Philadelphia. We went to the Final with the Oilers in 2006 and Flyers in 2010, overcoming a three-games-to-zero deficit in the second round.

But who would have thought after rooming with Scott in Salt Lake City, playing alongside him in the first game, we would wind up together in Anaheim and bring a Stanley Cup championship to California for the first time? Just one day, I wish I could skate like him.

Scott and I both ended up in Anaheim without warning. Scott signed as an unrestricted free agent with the Ducks to play with his brother, Rob, in 2005, 16 months after the pair won a world championship together for Canada. I followed Scott to Anaheim a year later, and in our first year together, we won a Stanley Cup to go with our gold medal from Salt Lake City five years earlier.

The three of us carpooled in the spring of 2007. Scott drove a Toyota Prius in those days. He would pick up Rob and me, and the three of us would talk about life and the game and joke around. It was the perfect way to prepare for the pressure of playoff hockey.

We won Olympic gold again in Vancouver in 2010. But I'm kind of jealous of Scott and how many trophies he has in his possession. He was our Conn Smythe Trophy winner in 2007 as the playoff MVP and won three Stanley Cup titles with New Jersey before arriving in Anaheim. He also won a Memorial Cup with the Kamloops Blazers in 1991–92, while my Peterborough Petes lost to the Sault Ste. Marie Greyhounds in the Memorial Cup final 12 months later.

I could not have imagined that nine years later, I would be in the Olympic Games. Growing up in Dryden, Ontario, I dreamed of winning a Stanley Cup. Olympic gold became a possibility in 1998 and a reality four years later. With Gretzky leading and talent like Lemieux, MacInnis, Niedermayer, Sakic, and Yzerman competing, we had a good feeling in Salt Lake City.

Winning gold was magical, and being part of one of Canada's most historic hockey moments was a privilege.

Chris Pronger played 18 seasons in the NHL, winning the Hart Memorial Trophy as NHL MVP for the 1999–2000 season and the Stanley Cup with the Anaheim Ducks in 2007. With Team Canada, Pronger won gold at the 2002 and 2010 Winter Olympics.

INTRODUCTION

My phone rang at approximately 9:40 PM on the evening of March 23, 2001. I was sitting at my desk inside the *Globe and Mail* newsroom in downtown Toronto. We were putting the final touches on the first edition. In my role as assistant sports editor back then, I oversaw the evening production. But with skillful night editors like Chuck Corley, Phil King, and Wayne Walters, I left most of the decisions up to these capable newspapermen.

The area code 403 phone number was familiar. It belonged to Brad Pascall, then the media relations guru for Hockey Canada. I found it odd that Pascall would be calling so late. He had stickhandled his way through a long day. As part of the NHL's attempt to whip up publicity and interest for the 2002 Winter Olympics in Salt Lake City, Hockey Canada introduced its first eight players to the men's team's roster.

"Timmy, do you have a minute?" Pascall asked.

"Yeah, sure, of course I do," I replied. "What's up?"

"Wayne Gretzky is here," Pascall said. "He wants to say hi and congratulate you."

"For what?" I asked.

"You were the only guy to get the eight players correctly," Pascall answered.

I was surprised. Most hockey writers across Canada took their shot. Seven were no-brainers in defencemen Rob Blake and Scott Niedermayer as well as forwards Paul Kariya, Mario Lemieux, Joe Sakic, and Steve Yzerman. The tricky part was deciding who would be the eighth member.

Every time somebody took a shot at predicting the elite eight, either Gretzky or Hockey Canada president Bob Nicholson would shake their heads from side to side. I didn't have any insider knowledge or anything. But I did notice that every list omitted Owen Nolan, then of the San Jose Sharks.

I liked Nolan. He was born in Belfast, Northern Ireland, although his family moved to Canada when he was seven months old. He played a belligerent game. But he liked to have fun, too. Playing in front of his home fans in the 1997 NHL All-Star Game, Nolan scored a hat trick.

His third goal arrived in style in the third period against the goalie Dominik Hasek, who would give Canada such a difficult time in the semifinals of the 1998 Nagano Olympics 12 months later. The Sharks right wing skated in on a breakaway, pointed to the left side. Ding went Nolan's wrister, off the post and in for his hat trick.

He also scored the gold-medal-clinching goal in Canada's 2–1 win against Sweden in the final of the 1997 IIHF World Championship in Helsinki, Finland. It was one of the few bright spots Canadian NHLers managed on the international stage in the mid- to late 1990s. They lost the 1996 World Cup of Hockey and exited early against Hasek and the Czech Republic at the 1998 Winter Games.

Besides liking Nolan's personality and style of play, he was also one of agent Mike Barnett's favourites. Barnett just happened to be Gretzky's close friend and his representative during his playing days. Barnett had ample time to influence No. 99 and make a case for Nolan, Barnett's All-Star client. So, Nolan it was.

"Congratulations," Gretzky said after Pascall handed him the phone. "I think you're the only guy who got it right. I just wanted to call and get to know you, and I want to give you my numbers so you can get ahold of me down the road. If I can help you in any way, don't hesitate to call me."

Gretzky gave me his home number and his Blackberry digits, as well as his email address. I didn't feel the need to call him until the Toronto Maple Leafs and New Jersey Devils advanced to play against each other in the second round of the 2001 Stanley Cup playoffs a few weeks later. The matchup pitted Maple Leafs goalie Curtis Joseph against his Devils counterpart Martin Brodeur.

I rang Gretzky to see how much he and the Canadian Olympic management team would focus on the second-round series. How much would Brodeur's and Joseph's play determine their status on the Canadian Olympic team nine months later in Salt Lake City? Gretzky ignored my messages.

One of my first brushes with the Great One was back in the spring of 1997. It turned out to be such an enjoyable assignment because the hockey was massively entertaining between his Rangers and Brodeur and the Devils in the second round of the Stanley Cup playoffs. Ten days in Manhattan watching and reporting on Gretzky, Mark Messier, and Brian Leetch against Bobby Holik, Niedermayer, and Brodeur was quite a trip.

The Rangers won the series four games to one, but every game was tight. Brodeur and Rangers netminder Mike Richter were outstanding. Richter made 46 saves in the finale, a 2–1 road win in enemy territory for the Rangers. But the five games took a lot out of the aging New York club. The Rangers were no match for the Philadelphia

Flyers in the East final. Gretzky would play his final Stanley Cup postseason game that spring on May 25, 1997.

Less than two years later, during the penultimate weekend of the regular season, Gretzky's potential retirement became a massive story as the struggling Rangers played out their final three games of the season. Madison Square Garden network analyst John Davidson set in motion the possibility of Gretzky packing it in on *Hockey Night in Canada* on Saturday, April 10, 1999, during the "Satellite Hot Stove" segment during the second intermission.

"The people very close to Wayne, and I mean very close, feel there's a very strong possibility Sunday [April 18] will be the last time he plays," Davidson said during the broadcast.

I was working for the *Toronto Sun* back then. For the next two days, I chased this story. Finally, as I sat down for my first pint of Monday evening with colleague Al Strachan at the Madison Pub, the phone rang. Alanna, the bartender, said it was for me.

My contact with the New York Rangers confirmed No. 99 would play his final game against the Pittsburgh Penguins at Madison Square Garden on Sunday. Another source earlier in the day had told me about the uncustomary number of tickets that Gretzky had purchased for the season finale.

"Gretzky 99% Gone; Great One Likely to Play Last One on Sunday" was the headline in the *Toronto Sun* the next morning. Even though my friend Larry Brooks also wrote a similar piece in the *New York Post* that day, you don't sleep until a big story like that plays out.

No. 99 kept a low profile for the next two days. He did state after the Rangers practice on Wednesday, before the team boarded its charter for a flight to Ottawa to play the Senators the following night, that his decision "won't be today or tomorrow."

My heart sank. But then, after the Rangers-Senators game, Gretzky insinuated the end was near.

"All indications are obviously pointing in that direction," Gretzky said after a 2–2 tie.

"It's an emotional time…. It's going to take a miracle tomorrow morning."

The next morning, he confirmed he was hanging up his skates at 38 and after 20 NHL seasons. "My gut, my heart, tells me this is the right time," Gretzky said.

Phew. That episode was over. But my brushes with Gretzky did not end there or after that March 2001 phone call. The next time he was extremely pissed at me.

Four months after the Gretzky-guided Canadian team claimed gold in Salt Lake City in 2002, the Phoenix Coyotes signed unrestricted free agent Tony Amonte. Yes, the same Amonte who scored the game-winning goal for the United States against Canada in the 1996 World Cup of Hockey, and the same Amonte who put the U.S. ahead 1–0 early in the gold medal game at the Olympics.

Gretzky was in his second full season as the managing partner in Phoenix. The Amonte signing was unexpected, shocking. He agreed to a four-year, $24 million deal with the financially challenged Coyotes, a team that had dumped the salaries of marquee talent like Jeremy Roenick and Keith Tkachuk in previous seasons.

A few weeks after the Amonte deal was signed, sealed, and delivered, Gretzky was in Edmonton playing at his annual charity golf tournament at the Jack Nicklaus–designed Northern Bear Golf Course.

Reporters queried him about the escalating salaries in the game. Gretzky was concerned. He worried about small-market teams competing with big spenders like the Detroit Red Wings, who a few months earlier had won the Stanley Cup for the third time in six years.

"We've got to keep the history of our game," Gretzky remarked. "We need to keep Edmonton and Calgary and Ottawa in the league and teams like Pittsburgh and Phoenix. It is no secret it is a little more difficult for the small-market teams than the big-market teams. Hopefully, that will change."

I was helping out the *Sporting News* magazine on a freelance basis that summer. The gig called for the occasional opinion piece. I didn't particularly appreciate that Gretzky, the hockey executive, seemed to forget about his time as Gretzky, the player.

I always supported the players. I worked for the NHLPA for 10½ months as its media relations director in 2000 before returning to the newspaper business at the *Globe and Mail*.

In 1996, after his brief stint with the St. Louis Blues concluded, Gretzky became an unrestricted free agent. He had spurned a three-year, $15 million offer to stay in St. Louis. As expected, he was courted by big-market teams like the Toronto Maple Leafs, Vancouver Canucks, and New York Rangers. The latter two clubs competed in a memorable seven-game Stanley Cup Final in 1994.

Gretzky, then 35, wound up signing a two-year, $8 million contract with the Rangers to reunite with Mark Messier, his old friend from their days with the Edmonton Oilers.

I was critical of Gretzky changing his tune now that he was a club executive. But with the collective bargaining agreement back then set to expire on September 15, 2004, it was clear that NHL commissioner Gary Bettman had asked a handful of hockey power brokers to paint a doom-and-gloom financial picture.

Gretzky was not amused with my column. He had his handlers phone the *Sporting News* to protest. The magazine's editors offered Gretzky's guys space for rebuttal. But they had gone silent.

I must admit I was worried when I began the process of writing this book as to whether No. 99 would make himself available for an interview. He never did warm up to me after the summer of 2002 in the encounters we had with each other.

But Gretzky did call me after repeated attempts to lasso him for this book. He was interview subject No. 21 of 35. He was charming and open.

I have a theory when it comes to how accommodating most hockey players are with the sporting press. Decades ago, superstars like Gordie Howe and Jean Beliveau set the standard with their class and friendliness. There have been exceptions, but this pleasantness from hockey players has been carried on by the likes of Bobby Orr, Gretzky, and Dale Hawerchuk and skated along to Sidney Crosby.

In discussing the 2002 Olympic Games with players, members of the coaching staff, and management team, it was apparent how much Gretzky was responsible for this group's golden success. This book became a love letter to the Great One, another rather massive accomplishment in his brilliant career.

"The passion from Gretz was the difference," Martin Brodeur told me when I asked him why the team in 2002 won and a very talented team in 1998 wound up without a medal.

But Gretzky's passion for putting Canada back on top is only part of what makes 2002 a compelling tale. How did the team keep its cool after such a slow start? There were the comeback stories of Theo Fleury, Paul Kariya, Michael Peca, and Eric Lindros. There was veteran wisdom from Mario Lemieux and Al MacInnis. The heart of Ryan Smyth to make the team. There was Joe Sakic's brilliance.

Scott Niedermayer added yet another championship. Steve Yzerman, Lemieux, and Brendan Shanahan played through pain. There was the youthful exuberance from Jarome Iginla, Simon Gagne, and Eric Brewer.

The time together for this group was thrilling, from summer camp to being presented with their championship rings in October 2002. Paul Henderson, Phil Esposito, and Bobby Clarke produced an unforgettable victory because of the comeback in the Summit Series against the Soviet Union, and it was the first of its kind. The 2002 Canadian Olympic team enjoyed a similar rally to end a long drought. Both wins sent Canadians into the streets to celebrate.

If you're like me, you want to know what makes a team like this tick. What did the players feel was essential to their Salt Lake City success? This group was incredibly transparent in discussing what transpired 20 years ago. It was evident they wanted to share the experience, right down to who they roomed with in the Athletes Village.

So, let's begin there, with the room assignments. Ryan Smyth, Eric Brewer, and Ed Jovanovski were the only ones who had to triple up. Adam Foote was with his Colorado Avalanche teammate Rob Blake. Chris Pronger roomed with his future Anaheim Ducks teammate Scott Niedermayer. Veterans Al MacInnis and Joe Nieuwendyk paired together. Paul Kariya–Curtis Joseph, Michael Peca–Owen Nolan, Theo Fleury–Joe Sakic, Simon Gagne–Martin Brodeur, Jarome Iginla–Ed Belfour, and Brendan Shanahan–Eric Lindros were other bunkmate combinations.

And who roomed with captain Mario Lemieux? Steve Yzerman is the answer.

CHAPTER 1

Pre-Olympic Pressure

Steve Nash woke up early on the morning of Sunday, February 24, 2002. He was in the sixth season of his Hall of Fame career, fourth with the Dallas Mavericks.

The night before the Canadian men's hockey team's gold medal match against the United States, Nash scored a team-leading 28 points in the Mavericks' 111–97 win at home against the Sacramento Kings. Nash and the Mavericks did not play again until another outing in Dallas on Tuesday, this time against the visiting Memphis Grizzlies.

So Nash, raised in Victoria, British Columbia, had arranged to borrow the private jet of Mavericks owner Mark Cuban to fly to Salt Lake City to attend the historic hockey game and what he hoped would be a victory for his home and native land.

Securing a ticket to the final event was another matter, however. The E Center, an Olympic-sized ice surface venue in the West Valley City suburb on the outskirts of Salt Lake City, only had seating capacity for 8,599.

Thankfully for Nash, he was put in touch with a Toronto-based ticket broker named Ervil Digiusto. The self-proclaimed "Canada's most trusted ticket broker since 1983" attended all the big sporting events in North America, and he was there in Salt Lake City plying his trade. Digiusto had dealt with VIPs in his career, but Nash was the biggest celebrity to contact him. He wound up spending $10,000 for a few tickets that Sunday.

"It obviously was a huge deal with Canada having gone 50 years without a gold medal in men's hockey," Canadian centre and tournament MVP Joe Sakic said. "We knew the entire country back home was with us, and then to meet Canadians like Steve Nash, somebody I admired so much, at the game, it took on a heightened importance."

Hockey Hall of Fame play-by-play announcer Bob Cole skillfully captured the importance. The Newfoundlander had a knack for rising to the occasion. When Paul Henderson scored his last-minute series-winner in the eight-game 1972 Summit Series against the Soviet Union, Cole seized the moment on CBC radio.

"Henderson! The team powers over the boards. They're mobbing Henderson. They're hugging Henderson. And Kenny Dryden, I've never seen a goaltender do that—skating from one end of the ice to the other, over 200 feet, all the way. And team officials are over the boards. Henderson has got to be the hero of the entire nation now, 34 seconds left. They have a 6–5 lead. Can they hang on?'"

Then there was the time the Soviet Red Army team hastily left the ice surface in the first period, upset with the physicality of the Philadelphia Flyers in this exhibition game.

"They're going home," Cole said. "They're going home. Yeah, they're going home."

Another dandy was when Pittsburgh Penguins captain Mario Lemieux undressed Minnesota North Star Shawn Chambers and deked goalie Jon Casey in the second period of Game 2 of the 1991 Stanley Cup Final.

"Here's Lemieux. To centre. Penalty coming up. Look at Lemieux. Oh, my heavens. What a goal. What a move. Lemieux! Oh, baby!"

Cole knew he had to be at his best, once again, in February 2002. There was a captive coast-to-coast record television audience of 10.6 million tuned in back home in Canada. The number of viewers peaked to 12.6 million as the final seconds ticked off the clock. Canada was ready for a party.

Cole rolled out the red carpet, first with his call of Sakic's goal to give Canada a three-goal cushion with 80 seconds remaining. "Canada trying to hang on and get a break. It's gonna be a break. It is Joe Sakic...scores! Jee-O Sakic! Scores! And that makes it 5–2, Canada. Surely, that's gotta be it."

The goal was enough. The legendary *Hockey Night in Canada* announcer then delivered his memorable closing words as the Canadian bench went crazy, as team executive director Wayne Gretzky hugged his management team of Kevin Lowe and Steve Tambellini as well as Hockey Canada president Bob Nicholson up in the stands.

"Now after 50 years, it's time for Canada to stand up and cheer. Stand up and cheer, everybody! The Olympics Salt Lake City, 2002, men's ice hockey gold medal: Canada!"

Like he has so many times in his career, Cole found the right words as Sakic and Co. closed in on their golden moment.

"It's the strangest things, these calls," Cole said. "I don't plan them. I don't script them. But they must be somewhere swimming around in my head. One of the many lessons [hockey's first great announcer] Foster Hewitt taught me was to follow the ups and downs of a game with the tone or pitch of my voice."

Cole was known for his intonation. You could listen to a game he called with your back to the television and know when to turn around.

For the next several weeks and months, moved Canadians would approach Cole with kind words and stories about his golden call.

"The one I will always recall is seeing [then Canadian] Prime Minister Jean Chretien being interviewed on television on how he celebrated," Cole said. "And what did he say? He stood up and cheered, just like I suggested."

Ken Hitchcock, one of the Canadian assistant coaches, ran into Cole a few months later and applauded the announcer's work on the gold medal final.

"He told me that whenever he's having a tough day he pops in the gold medal tape and watches the final few minutes," Cole said. "So I asked [CBC producer] Kathy [Broderick] for a copy. The first time I watched it I had goosebumps. I have goosebumps just talking about it now."

Cole's final dispatch from Salt Lake City sent millions of Canadians streaming into the streets, onto Granville in Vancouver, Whyte Avenue in Edmonton, the corner of Portage and Main in Winnipeg, Yonge in Toronto, Rue Ste-Catherine in Montreal, and George in Mr. Cole's hometown of St. John's.

Every Canadian knows where they were the day Lemieux and the lads ended the 50-year Olympic gold medal drought. But how many Canadians can tell the story of how Wayne Gretzky called to congratulate them for another significant victory on that golden afternoon?

Canadian PGA Tour player Ian Leggatt has one of the more unique stories from Sunday, February 24, 2002. A sports nut and decent hockey player back in his youth growing up in Cambridge, Ontario, Leggatt was a 12-hour drive away to the south of Salt Lake City, competing at the PGA Tour stop in Tucson, Arizona.

The Tucson tournament has a rich history. Past champions include Lee Trevino, Phil Mickelson, and Johnny Miller, as well as the late Canadian legend George Knudson. Leggatt was 36 years old and had yet to win on the PGA Tour. But just like something special was happening with the Canadian Olympic team 12 hours north, Leggatt's time was about to arrive.

A 68–71 start placed Leggatt three strokes inside the cut line. The day before Canada was to meet the United States in the gold medal match, Leggatt checked in with an impressive seven-under-par 65 to move himself into contention. He was in the third-last group on the final day.

Before his final-round tee time, Leggatt bumped into fellow Canadian golfer Glen Hnatiuk of Selkirk, Manitoba (near Winnipeg). The pair were fired up about Canada's chances against the U.S. that day, as well as their own possibilities in Tucson. Hnatiuk was playing five groups before his fellow countryman.

The Canadian-U.S. game already had begun by the time Leggatt teed off in the final round. Golf Channel on-course reporter Jerry Foltz provided periodic updates to Leggatt and his caddy as his final round progressed.

Word eventually filtered from Foltz to Leggatt that Canada had won gold. He remembers being on the 12th hole when the news of Canada's hockey win was delivered. He saw Hnatiuk on the 16th green a minute or two later, and the two feigned a high five from a distance.

Leggatt progressed to card a final-round 64, the low round of the day, for a two-shot victory over David Peoples and Loren Roberts. Hnatiuk finished in a tie for 25th.

On any other day, Leggatt's impressive win would have been celebrated with front-page headlines on sports sections across Canada. But instead, his victory was muted.

"I didn't realize until the tournament was over the significance of winning that day," Leggatt said. "Sure, my win would have been a big story back home on any other day. But I don't mind being attached in a neat way to such a historic win."

Leggatt once read an article about two-time Canadian Open winner Bruce Lietzke, whose first win also was in Tucson. Lietzke relayed that one of the best feelings he ever experienced in his career was the drive in his Trans Am from Tucson to the next tournament at Pebble Beach, California, a trip that took him two days to make.

"I actually started driving Sunday in a Trans Am Firebird by myself," Lietzke said. "I plugged in an 8-track tape of Lynard Skynard.

"That is the closest I have ever come to heaven without a doubt—maximum volume; Lynyrd Skynyrd on the 8-track, and just having won my first tournament. If you don't know the circumstances, I made an 82-foot putt to beat Gene Littler in a playoff on the fourth playoff hole, my first tournament victory as a pro, that is it for me. That is the greatest thrill in golf for me. But it wasn't the golf. It wasn't the putt. It was me, patting myself on the back for the next two, three hours and listening to Lynyrd Skynyrd."

Leggatt knew what Lietzke described. After the trophy presentation to the Canadian and his interview sessions concluded, Leggatt hopped in his car to make the two-hour drive back to his Scottsdale-area home. His voice mailbox was full. But as he listened to the messages on his drive, he heard Gretzky's voice. The two knew each other from some charity golf events. The Great One found time during the gold medal celebrations to congratulate the golfer.

"That was kind of cool," Leggatt said. "I also flew to Miami for the next stop on Monday and that week Tiger Woods congratulated me. All of a sudden, you go from just a PGA Tour player to a PGA Tour winner.

"The neat thing for me was eight years later in 2010 I got to attend Canada's gold medal game in Vancouver. I sat five rows up from the ice with [Canadian two-time World champion curler] John Kawaja. We flew back to California after the game on Wayne Gretzky's plane."

Also nestled in the E Center crowd on the day the Canadian men ended the 50-year gold medal dry spell were four of the dozen living members of the 1952 Edmonton Mercurys, 50 years to the day the Mercurys became the last team to represent Canada and win gold at the Olympic Winter Games in Oslo, Norway.

In a Labatt brewery promotion, Donald "Choo-Choo" Gauf, Billie Dawe, William Gibson, and Eric Paterson, the backup goalie to the outstanding Ralph Hansch, were brought to Salt Lake City to reminisce about their victory five decades prior and to witness whether or not Lemieux, Sakic, and the boys would end the half-century Olympic championship drought.

The Mercurys were a team sponsored by Jim Christiansen's Waterloo Mercury Lincoln dealership in Edmonton. The team was formed in 1949 and many of the players worked for Christiansen. One of the exceptions was Hansch, who was a firefighter. The Mercurys successfully revved their engine with a world championship crown in 1950 at the famed Wembley Arena in London, England.

The Oslo Games was a nine-team tournament and consisted of an eight-game round-robin. According to the Canadian Encyclopedia, Canada entered the final day on Sunday, February 24, 1952, with six wins and a tie, one point in front of the United States, with six victories and a loss.

Edmonton enjoyed a 2–0 lead, only to watch the U.S. draw even. Choo-Choo put Canada in front 3–2 in the third period, but the Red, White, and Blue tied the game for a second and final time with two minutes to play. Canada had another gold medal with a 7–0–1 record to finish a point ahead of its North American rivals.

But who knew that would be the final Canadian men's hockey team Olympic gold medal for a long, long time. The Canadians had dominated the hockey competition, winning the first six of seven

Olympic tournaments. They had a combined record of 37–1–3 and outscored the opposition 403 to 34.

There was gold with the Winnipeg Falcons in Antwerp, Belgium, in 1920, followed by the Toronto Granites in Chamonix, France, in 1924; University of Toronto Grads in St. Moritz, Switzerland, in 1928; the Winnipeg Hockey Club in Lake Placid, New York, in 1932; the Ottawa RCAF Flyers in St. Moritz in 1948, and finally, the Mercurys in Oslo.

The only hiccup for the Canadian side came in 1936. The Halifax Wolverines won the 1935 Allan Cup title and therefore were chosen to represent Canada at the Olympics in Garmisch-Partenkirchen, Germany. But the Wolverines disbanded the following season. Therefore, the team they defeated in the Allan Cup in a two-game final, the Port Arthur Bearcats, instead represented Canada.

The Bearcats invited four of the former members from the Halifax team to play in Germany, but the ex-Wolverines declined after their request to have their travel costs covered was dismissed.

In Garmisch-Partenkirchen, Port Arthur suffered a 2–1 loss to Great Britain in the key round-robin game. Great Britain had 11 members who were Canadian born and raised.

A massive reason why Canada went 50 years between Olympic gold medals was the emergence of the Big Red Machine, the Soviet Union national team. A Russian league didn't exist until 1946, and the Soviets didn't send a national team to the world championship until 1954.

The Russians, however, made an immediate impact. They upset Canada, represented by the East York Lyndhursts, 7–2 in the decisive game. The Soviets continued on to win Olympic gold in 1956, 1964, 1968, 1972, 1976, 1984, 1988 and, if you include, 1992, when the Unified team was the victor. The United Team was put into place for the 1992 Olympic Games in Albertville, France. The Soviet Union officially dissolved at midnight on New Year's Eve 1991. The former Soviet republics of Armenia, Belarus, Kazakhstan, Russia, Ukraine, and Uzbekistan combined in the short term to make up the Unified Team two months later at the Winter Games in the Auvergne-Rhone Alps.

On only two occasions between 1956 and 1988 did the Soviets or the former Soviet Union not strike gold in an Olympic Games. They settled for silver in 1980 in Lake Placid and bronze 20 years earlier in Squaw Valley, California. Instead, the Americans went two-for-two on home soil to mess up the Russian domination, a fact that was not lost on Wayne Gretzky and played a role when he delivered his passionate rant in support of his players at the midway point of the tournament in Salt Lake City.

The Canadians weren't totally absent from the medal picture after 1952. The Kitchener-Waterloo Dutchmen, who were the Canadian Olympic representatives in 1956 and 1960, settled for bronze and silver, respectively, in their visits to the Winter Games. Martin Brodeur's father, Denis, was a goalie for the Dutchmen in 1956.

The 1960 Olympics was the final time Canada was represented by a senior amateur team in the Winter Games. Father David Bauer had established the Canadian national team in time for the 1964 Olympics in Innsbruck, Austria.

In 1968, at Grenoble, France, Canada was thumped 5–0 by the Soviets and upset 2–1 by Finland. The two defeats dropped Canada into third.

Canada did not participate in the 1976 Olympics when the Winter Games returned to Innsbruck. The Canadian Amateur Hockey Association was upset with the International Ice Hockey Federation (IIHF) for not allowing Canada to use semi-professional players on its national team. The situation already appeared unfair with the Soviet national team training together for 12 months a year.

As a result, Canada did not compete in the springtime world championships from 1970 to 1976 nor the 1976 Winter Olympics.

Canada, instead, decided to nourish its appetite for best-on-best international hockey with the eight-game Summit Series against the Soviet Union in 1972 and the development of the Canada Cup in 1976. There also were Canada Cup tournaments in 1981, 1984, 1987, and 1991. This tournament morphed into the World Cup of Hockey, so far sporadically contested in 1996, 2004, and 2016.

Canada wasn't devoid of magical hockey moments after the Edmonton Mercurys' golden effort in 1952. Paul Henderson's last-second, crease-crashing goal to give Canada a win in the Summit Series sent the country into a mad frenzy. Darryl Sittler's overtime thriller for Canada in the inaugural Canada Cup provided another classic ending four years later.

There also were the late-game heroics in 1987, 15 years after Henderson's historic goal. On September 15, 1987, with the best-of-three final between the Soviet Union and Canada even at 1–1 and the deciding game tied 5–5, Canada's Dale Hawerchuk won a key faceoff in his own end. Lemieux swooped in to collect the puck. He eluded a Russian player and poked the puck to Gretzky, who skated down the left boards. Employing teammate Larry Murphy as a decoy, No. 99 found Lemieux trailing and fired a wrist shot into the top right corner for the winner with 86 ticks left on the score clock hanging above centre ice at Copps Coliseum in Hamilton, Ontario.

The underrated Steve Larmer provided the grand ending in the 1991 Canada Cup with his tournament-clinching shorthanded breakaway goal late in the third period of the final against the United

States. It wasn't as dramatic a goal as Henderson's or Lemieux's, but it certainly provided to be a vengeful ending for Canada.

In the best-of-three opener, U.S. defenceman Gary Suter slammed Wayne Gretzky from behind and into the boards. The dirty play knocked No. 99 out of the tournament and instantly made Suter enemy No. 1 in Canada, a role he would reprise before the 1998 Olympics.

Suter was the opponent Larmer stripped of the puck for his breakaway backhand through the legs of U.S. goalie Mike Richter. Larmer led the 1991 tournament with six goals in eight games.

The NHL finally followed the NBA's lead and decided to participate in the 1998 Olympics, six years after Michael Jordan, Magic Johnson, and rest of the United States Dream Team dominated for the first time in Barcelona.

There were high hopes in Canada that there would finally be an Olympic men's gold to celebrate. But there were close calls before the NHL's decision to join the Olympic movement.

There was 1960. Canada appeared on the right track after opening with victories against Sweden, Japan, Germany, and Czechoslovakia by a combined score of 40–3. Canada also finished with another win against Sweden and an 8–5 favourable decision against Russia.

But in the middle of the round-robin tournament, U.S. goalie Jack McCartan handed Canada its only blemish. McCartan was incredible against Canada with 39 saves. In the 2–1 loss, Canada didn't beat McCartan until Dutchmen Floyd "Butch" Martin set up James Connelly with less than seven minutes to play.

To add to the disappointment for local fans of the Dutchmen, McCartan wound up playing the following season for the Kitchener-Waterloo Beavers of the Eastern Professional Hockey League. One of his teammates with the Beavers was Don Cherry, a future Jack Adams winner as NHL Coach of the Year for the 1975–76 Boston Bruins and later the colourful star of *Hockey Night in Canada*'s "Coach's Corner" segment.

"Jack was such a good guy and a terrific goalie," said Cherry, who recalled how McCartan pleaded for Cherry to sell him his 1957 Oldsmobile.

Another Beavers teammate, Bob Sabourin, was a used-car salesman in the offseason and told Cherry—"Grapes"—he could work out a deal for another automobile for him. Finally, Cherry gave in.

"I remember the price—800 bucks," Cherry said. "I knew the transmission was about to go on the car. I told Jack, but he did not seem to care. He drove it back home [to Minnesota] after the season, and his dad fell in love with the car."

But, of course, there wasn't much life left in the old Oldsmobile. It didn't take long for the car to be junked because, as Cherry predicted, the transmission took its last breath.

A few months later, Cherry was back in Springfield, Massachusetts, with the Indians of the American Hockey League. He was preparing for an exhibition game when McCartan, who was with the opposition before being demoted down to the Beavers for a second campaign, barrelled into the Indians' dressing room.

"He was upset," Cherry said. "He called me every name in the book, even though I reminded him I warned him about the transmission."

The next close call for Canada at the Olympics arrived prior to the 1988 Winter Games in Calgary. In one of the more prestigious tournaments back then, Canadian national team head coach Dave King took his squad to Moscow to see how his group stacked up in the Izvestia Tournament in mid-December 1987.

Canada opened the six-country, round-robin tournament with a 3–2 loss to Sweden and a 3–1 win against Czechoslovakia to set up the game against the host country on December 19. The Soviets, who were less than three months removed from their devastating loss to Lemieux and Gretzky at the Canada Cup in Hamilton, jumped out to a 2–0 lead. They looked like they were on their way.

But late in the second period, Wally Schreiber pulled Canada within one with a timely wraparound goal. In the final 20 minutes, Canadian forward Ken Berry scored with a long shot, exposing the Soviets' weakness at the time, their goaltending. Then Berry, this time in close, scored the go-ahead goal with 11:11 remaining, and Canadian goalie Sean Burke closed the door like he did throughout the tournament.

"Whenever you pull off an upset like this you need pretty good goaltending," King said. "Sean gave us a chance because of how well he played."

The atmosphere in Luzhniki Arena, the same building in which Paul Henderson scored his iconic goal, was ugly that day in 1987. The home fans whistled their athletes off the ice. The Canadians were euphoric. But they still had two games to play, including the next day against West Germany.

Despite a sensational effort from West German goalie Josef "Beppo" Schlickenrieder, who stopped Schreiber and Marc Habscheid on breakaways and made his best save on Serge Boisvert from close range, Ken Yaremchuk managed to score the difference-maker with less than seven minutes to play in Canada's eventual 2–1 win. Two days later, the tournament victory was completed with a 4–1 win against Finland.

Burke recalled forward Gord Sherven and defenceman Randy Gregg had purchased a bottle of champagne on the black market the night before the tournament finale for a memorable dressing room celebration.

"The things you learn the guys did afterward," King said with a chuckle. "The coach is always the last to know.

"It certainly was a terrific accomplishment. I still see lots of guys from that team and it doesn't take long for our conversation to turn to 1987. It was a true David beats Goliath sort of accomplishment, and it took place in a historic building."

My former *Globe and Mail* colleague Eric Duhatschek dubbed the unexpected win "Canada's Miracle on Ice." But the victory had its cost. It woke up the rest of the hockey world to how well this Canadian team could play. King and his players were not to be taken lightly in Calgary, Alberta, for the 1988 Olympics. They finished fourth.

The Big Red Machine, boasting the best five-man unit in hockey at the time with Igor Larionov between Vladimir Krutov and Sergei Makarov up front and Viacheslav Fetisov and Alexei Kasatonov on defence, blanked Canada 5–0 in the final round portion of the 1988 Olympics.

King and Burke fared much better in Albertville four years later. They opened by winning four of their first five games in the first round. Canada's lone loss was a narrow 5–4 decision to the Unified Team. In the playoff round, Canada defeated Germany in a 4–3 shootout win in the quarterfinals and a 4–2 victory against the former Czechoslovakia in the semifinals three days later.

The big win put Canada into the gold medal game against the Unified Team. Eric Lindros, who then was a few days shy of his 19th birthday, and the Canadians held their opponents to a goalless tie through 40 minutes. But the Unified Team scored on Burke early in the final 20 minutes and again with four minutes remaining. Chris Lindberg made it close for Canada before the Unified Team scored a final late-game goal for a 3–1 victory.

"They deserved to win," Burke said. "You need 21 guys playing the best game of their lives to beat them. We came close to doing that."

Two years later in Lillehammer, Norway, the Canadians experienced another close shave, this time under head coach Tom Renney. They opened with wins against Italy and France, as expected. But after a 3–3 draw with rival United States, Canada suffered a setback with a 3–1 loss to Slovakia. Canada did, however, rebound with a 3–2 win against Peter Forsberg and Sweden before heading for the playoff round.

A 19-year-old Paul Kariya scored in overtime to eliminate the Czech Republic in the quarterfinals. After falling behind 2–0 against Finland, Canada scored five straight times to hang on for a 5–3 win in the semifinals.

In the gold medal final, Canada enjoyed a 2–1 lead against Sweden after Derek Mayer of Rossland, British Columbia, scored midway through the second period. But Forsberg set up Magnus Svensson for a power-play goal with 1:49 remaining in regulation time.

The championship game could not be decided in overtime and evolved to a shootout. Petr Nedved, a Czech who gained his Canadian citizenship, and Kariya scored for Canada in the first five rounds, but Svensson and Forsberg countered with goals for Sweden. In the second extra round, Kariya failed to beat Sweden's Tommy Salo.

The left-shot Forsberg fooled Canadian goalie Corey Hirsch with a fake to his forehand and reached back around the goaltender to slide a one-hand-on-the-stick backhand past Hirsch's outstretched glove hand. The shootout winner provided Sweden with its first Olympic men's hockey gold medal. To commemorate the victory, the Scandinavian country issued a postage stamp that captured the moment.

Nineteen months later, another historic moment occurred when the International Olympic Committee (IOC), the IIHF, the NHL Players' Association, and the NHL agreed to the game's best playing in the 1998 Winter Olympics in Nagano. Immediately, hockey fans felt with players like Gretzky, Sakic, Steve Yzerman, Raymond Bourque, and Patrick Roy suiting up, Canada would strut its stuff and finally end the madness by winning its first Olympic gold in hockey since 1952.

Gretzky and Co. certainly appeared to be a team of championship destiny. They reeled off sound victories in the preliminary round, 5–0 versus Belarus, 3–2 against Sweden, and 4–1 over the United States. It was on to the quarterfinals, and once again Canada looked as solid as gold with a 4–1 win against Kazakhstan.

The semifinals held a date with all-world goalie Dominik Hasek and the Czech Republic. Millions of Canadians stayed up to watch the semifinal game, which took place in the early morning hours.

Like Hasek, Canada's Roy had been excellent, too. He had gone four-for-four with only four goals allowed, while Hasek had surrendered five goals in four games, including a 2–1 defeat to Russia in the preliminary round. Hasek was in his prime, in the middle of winning the Vezina Trophy three consecutive times in 1996–97, 1997–98, and 1998–99.

He wasn't that busy in regulation time because of the Czechs' speedy and smothering defence-first system. Canada was stymied at every turn, and Roy kept his team in the game.

It took 49 minutes, 46 seconds for the first goal. Czech defenceman Jiri Slegr beat Roy on the stick side with a hard drive from the left point. Time was running out. But finally, Canada broke through the Czech wall. Canadian captain Eric Lindros dug the puck out from along the boards and found Trevor Linden. The latter's shot changed direction deflecting off a defender's stick. Canada now pulled even with only 63 seconds remaining in regulation time.

Linden would not have been on the ice had Canada's best player, Sakic, not been injured. He missed the semifinal after injuring his knee in the quarterfinal outing against Kazakhstan.

Sakic's absence severely hindered Canada's chances of skating into the gold medal final. The Canadians needed his deft touch around the net and would need his offensive skill if the game advanced to a shootout.

In the meantime, Linden's goal gave Canada a spark. Hasek wasn't that busy in regulation time as his teammates snuffed out Canada's attack. But in the 10-minute overtime period, Hasek was forced to make brilliant stops on Linden, Joe Nieuwendyk, and defenceman Adam Foote.

The game moved into the dreaded shootout. If facing the best goaltender in the world wasn't enough for Canada after Theo Fleury was stopped by a sprawled-out Hasek, Robert Reichel of the New York Islanders scored on the Czech's first attempt that bounded in off the post on Roy's stick side.

Bourque was up next, but his shot deflected off Hasek's catching arm and over the net. Roy countered with a glove save on Martin Rucinsky. It was on to Round 3. Nieuwendyk was Canada's third shooter. He tried to deke with a backhand, but on the beat-up ice surface the puck rolled on Nieuwendyk and his shot travelled wide.

Roy stopped Pavel Patera's five-hole attempt to keep Canada's hopes alive. It was Lindros' turn. He cruised in on Hasek with speed and tried to deke the Czech with a backhand to the goalie's stick side. Hasek rolled over on his back, swung his arm around, and got a piece of the puck to deflect Lindros' shot off the post.

Jaromir Jagr had a chance to end the game, but he also hit the post. That left the drama up to Brendan Shanahan. Like Nieuwendyk and Lindros, Shanahan attempted a deke. But he went to his forehand and ran out of room.

As Hasek was mobbed by his teammates, Lindros and Linden chased down Shanahan to console him. The Canadian players skated around in their end, waiting to shake the hands of their opponents. But there was one Canadian player missing—Wayne Gretzky. The Great One remained on the bench, lips pursed, looking dejected and in disbelief.

It was a gloomy snapshot ending to his one and only shot at Olympic gold as a player. Immediately, in Canada, head coach Marc Crawford's decision not to employ Gretzky as one of the shooters for the shootout was vehemently questioned. How could Crawford keep the game's greatest offensive players tethered to the bench? For that matter, why wasn't Steve Yzerman one of the choices?

The coach stood by his selections, saying his only regret was that the entire coaching staff should have sat down with the management team of Bobby Clarke, Bob Gainey, and Pierre Gauthier to hash out a final list.

Crawford later revealed he had the final say on the list of Canadian shooters. He did admit that before the game he asked Sakic and the training staff if he was healthy enough to participate in a shootout. Sakic was not fit enough.

The next day, the disheartened Canadians took the ice for their final appearance of the Nagano Games in the bronze medal game against Finland. Canada trailed 1–0 early when Gretzky's old linemate Jari Kurri scored. Rod Brind'Amour tied the game, but Jere Lehtinen put Finland back on top before the first period concluded.

Shanahan scored the lone goal in the middle frame on the power play thanks to a Gretzky pass, but Ville Peltonen checked in with the game's final goal early in the final period. The Canadian players excused their loss to Finland as a gold-or-bust situation. But two decades later some of the players felt they could have better absorbed a shootout loss with a bronze medal.

"Nagano, being so new, everything was so new," defenceman Rob Blake said. "The second time around you understand the process better, the shootout and things like that. We didn't fully understand what a silver or bronze medal would have meant.

"The way NHL players are brought up it's the big prize or nothing. The Olympic setting is different. It would have been something for those of us who played on both the 1998 and 2002 teams to have gold and bronze medals."

"If the outcome of [the bronze medal] game had been different, I think we could go home feeling better about ourselves," Yzerman added in Nagano. "Winning the bronze and losing only once, in a shootout, that would have been all right. But losing [against Finland] made it very disappointing."

It didn't seem to matter to the Canadians and their supporters that Hasek and the Czechs went on to win gold, holding Russia to only 20 shots on goal in a 1–0 victory in the championship game for their first Olympic gold medal in hockey.

"I've had some big wins and some tough losses, but the Czech game, no question, is one of the toughest losses I've ever experienced," Gretzky said after the bronze medal match. "We were in shock. It was one of those rare feelings we've gotten in our careers where we really didn't know what hit us."

Gretzky always has taken the high road when it comes to his omission in the shootout. So has Yzerman. They never publicly questioned Crawford and the coaching staff.

Meanwhile, Clarke, Gainey, Gauthier, and Crawford wanted to make sure that feeling didn't hit Canada the next time the world's best athletes assembled for a Winter Games. So they performed an internal audit on the inaugural Olympic experience for Canadian NHLers.

Clarke then sat down for a thorough debriefing session with Hockey Canada vice president Bob Nicholson, who would be promoted to president after Murray Costello retired.

Clarke admitted that among the management team's miscues were some personnel decisions. There were some developments that were out of his control, like Kariya being knocked out of the tournament a few weeks prior to the start. In a game between the Anaheim Ducks and Chicago Blackhawks on February 1, 1998, Blackhawks defenceman Gary Suter, who also played for the United States in Nagano, cross-checked Kariya in the face after the latter scored his second goal of the game.

Clarke held out hope and phoned Kariya a week before the Canadian team was to fly over to Japan, but Kariya was still bothered by the head injury. He endured a lengthy bout with post-concussion syndrome and missed the remainder of the season, including the playoffs. Mark Recchi, as a result, was tapped on the shoulder to replace Kariya.

Meanwhile, if Clarke had a do-over he never would have made Lindros, who was a few days shy of his 25th birthday in Nagano, the captain. That distinction and difficult task should have been bestowed on Gretzky.

"Lindros was a pretty young player at the time," Clarke said. "Gretzky was still the best player in the game. We made some mistakes and that was one of them."

Another regret was to omit Mark Messier from the team roster. Messier was 37 years old in February 1998 and his offensive numbers waned. But he played six more seasons after the Nagano Olympics.

"We didn't need a season out of Messier," Clarke said. "His play had slowed down that year, but we didn't need a season out of him, we needed a series out of him. His competitiveness, his leadership would have been a big boost."

That lack of leadership in Nagano was evident four years later in Salt Lake City because that was one of the top-drawer qualities of the 2002 team.

Canada also needed a boost to its offence. With all that talent on the Canadian side, the team managed to score only 18 goals in six games. But nine of those goals were scored in outings against Belarus and Kazakhstan. Canada checked in with only three goals in its final two games against the Czech Republic and Finland.

"We had put together a good team for NHL hockey, but not necessarily a good team for a short-term tournament," Clarke said. "We needed more players who could score. When you're in a tournament against the best goaltenders in the world, you need more offensive players."

Instead of simply selecting the best players, Clarke made sure some defensive players were included on his 1998 Canadian roster, players like Rob Zamuner and Shayne Corson.

Another mistake, Clarke provided, was leaving behind smooth-skating defenceman Scott Niedermayer. Instead, the Canadian management team selected hard-hitting New Jersey Devils teammate Scott Stevens. Niedermayer excelled in many areas of the game, but he was even better on the big ice surface because he skated so well.

"We also were missing Kariya," Clarke said. "We needed high, high-level players in a game that was playing fast. Niedermayer and Kariya are both capable of scoring and we ended up losing because we couldn't score.

"We had lots of good players, we played hard. We just ran into fucking Hasek."

There was one more piece of advice Clarke offered up to Nicholson, a recommendation that played a significant part in putting Canada back on the top step of the Olympic podium. Or as Bob Cole put it, "men's ice hockey gold medal: Canada!" It was Clarke who suggested who to put in charge of the 2002 team.

CHAPTER 2

ANOTHER
GRETZKY ASSIST

Wayne Gretzky was up and at 'em early most mornings in his career. His sunrise habit wasn't a case of wanting to get to the rink as soon as possible; it was more that he wanted to find someone to talk hockey. He wanted to discuss the game the night before, listen about a rising star or a slumping friend, or simply debate systems and philosophies.

In Nagano, part of his daily ritual was rising early and going down to the cafeteria in the Olympic Village to grab a morning coffee. This part of his routine resulted in his important involvement with Hockey Canada for the next Winter Games.

"It probably started in 1998 in the commissary of the Olympic Village in Nagano," Gretzky said. "I liked to get up really early and go get a coffee. Usually, Bobby Clarke and Bob Gainey would be sitting around talking about players and the direction of the way the game was going. It was a lot of fun for me to sit there and listen to a couple of guys who had been involved in the game for a long time.

"In my mind, I never thought about being a general manager of a team, but over the course of time it was Bobby Clarke who made the suggestion to Bob [Nicholson] to be the guy to take over the reins for 2002."

Clarke doesn't want any credit for his submission to Nicholson. Clarke didn't care that No. 99 didn't have any management experience, but he came away from those morning sessions with Gretzky knowing that he was a natural fit to run the next Canadian Olympic team.

"Gretzky was and has been everything you could ask for in a hockey man," Clarke said. "In my opinion, he is the best player to ever play the game. I know you might say Bobby Orr was the best, and I couldn't argue that. In my opinion, Gretzky was the best.

"But more than that, off the ice, he was such an intelligent hockey person. He knew what players made up a winning team. He was still the best player in the game. It was a necessity to have him involved in that team with Nicholson. [Gretzky] was easily the top hockey dog."

In 2002, Clarke was sitting in his Cherry Hill, New Jersey, home, pleased as punch as he watched Canada end its 50-year Olympic drought.

"I don't deserve any credit. I was just a hockey fan back then," said Clarke, a Hockey Hall of Fame member, one of the heroes for Canada at the 1972 Summit Series and back-to-back Stanley Cup champion with the Philadelphia Flyers in 1973–74 and 1974–75.

Clarke deserves praise for his recommendation of Gretzky. Nicholson deserves praise for listening.

"Do one thing," Clarke told Nicholson. "Have Gretzky involved in some way."

Nicholson recalled, "Clarke had been around, and he was amazed of the influence [Gretzky] had with the players and others."

There was one problem for Nicholson. It was two years after the disappointment of Nagano, and he didn't know whether the NHL players would be in Salt Lake City. Sure, like most, Nicholson felt the NHL could not pass up an opportunity to expand its reach with the Winter Games in North America. Besides, the NHL's inaugural participation in the Olympic Games in 1998 not only produced some entertaining hockey but a terrific story in the underdog Czech Republic winning its first Olympic gold in men's hockey.

Nevertheless, NHL commissioner Gary Bettman and IIHF president Rene Fasel were slow to resolve their differences to agree on NHL players being freed to compete at the 2002 Salt Lake City games. Finally, a new agreement was struck during the 2000 World Championship in St. Petersburg, Russia, on May 10. Shortly after, Nicholson made his first call to Gretzky to see if he was interested in any sort of role for the Canadian team.

"You always have a list, but Wayne was the first call I made," Nicholson said.

Gretzky's swan song NHL game was on Sunday, April 18, 1999. Seven months later, he was inducted into the Hockey Hall of Fame. His first post-playing career endeavour in hockey was when he took a 10 per cent ownership stake in the Phoenix Coyotes and became the club's managing partner and head of hockey operations.

Nicholson, meanwhile, had succeeded Murray Costello as president and CEO of Hockey Canada on July 1, 1998. Nicholson was in charge of the 1998 Canadian Olympic team, but Costello was in the final few months of his long tenure of running the Canadian Amateur Hockey Association, which became known as Hockey Canada.

"Everyone thought it was huge devastation in 1998, but that was a heckuva hockey team," Nicholson said. "We lost to a heckuva goalie in a shootout."

Could Gretzky push Canada over the hump? Like Clarke, Nicholson had a good feeling and liked what he heard from the Great One in the first phone call.

"Hey Wayne, would you liked to be involved?" Nicholson asked.

"Bob, I'd love to be involved, even if it's to be the stick boy," Gretzky replied.

A few days later, Nicholson flew to California to spend 48 hours discussing a lengthy list of subject matter. What role was the best fit for Gretzky? The good, bad, and ugly they experienced in Nagano. What was Gretzky's philosophy in building a team for the Olympics? What type of players did he want? What kind of leadership group did he want to construct? Who were some of the candidates for head coach? Who would be candidates to supplement the management team? How big should the coaching staff be? How many assistant managers should be named?

"I was really impressed with how much detail he had already thought about," Nicholson said.

Head coach obviously was an important matter to work out. It was a wide-open race. The last several Stanley Cup–winning head coaches were Canadian: Larry Robinson, Ken Hitchcock, Scott Bowman (twice), Marc Crawford, Jacques Lemaire, and Mike Keenan. Robinson was the interim bench boss when he steered the New Jersey Devils to the 1999–2000 NHL championship, only a few months prior to the Nicholson-Gretzky gathering.

Nicholson and Gretzky decided to each jot down their top-three candidates on a piece of paper. One name on Nicholson's list—but not on Gretzky's—was Pat Quinn.

Quinn and Nicholson knew each other well. Nicholson often used Quinn as a resource in various Hockey Canada programs.

Gretzky never played for the Big Irishman, as he was known. But as a member of the Edmonton Oilers, Los Angeles Kings, St. Louis Blues, and New York Rangers, Gretzky had endured many games against Quinn-coached clubs in Philadelphia, Los Angeles, Vancouver, and Toronto.

One of Quinn's best coaching jobs was with the 1998–99 Maple Leafs, also Gretzky's final season as a player. Quinn guided a team with three young blueliners in Bryan Berard, Tomas Kaberle, and Danny Markov all the way to the East final.

There also was the summer of 1996, when Gretzky was an unrestricted free agent. Quinn and Gretzky privately met in Seattle and talked hockey and a contract for 45 minutes. The two sides failed to come to an agreement when talks moved to the agent-ownership stage, but Gretzky departed with good vibrations about Quinn. He liked that Quinn had a simple system that encouraged an up-tempo skating and puck movement game.

The possibility of Quinn coaching Canada began trending in Gretzky's mind after a round of golf with Nicholson and Gretzky's neighbour, former NHLer Russ Courtnall. Briefly the two were teammates on the New York Rangers, and Courtnall was with the Canucks when Vancouver almost signed Gretzky. The Great One and Courtnall had homes on the Jack Nicklaus signature Sherwood Country Club.

After the round, Nicholson, Courtnall and Gretzky retired to the men's grill in the clubhouse for lunch. The subject of head coach was broached. Gretzky showed Courtnall a list of four names: Joel Quenneville, Jacques Martin, Ken Hitchcock, and Pat Quinn. Gretzky then asked Courtnall for his opinion.

"That's easy," Courtnall replied. "There's only one—Pat Quinn."

Courtnall played for some reputable coaches in Pat Burns in Montreal, Bob Gainey in Dallas, and Larry Robinson in Los Angeles. Quinn was the Canucks general manager when he acquired Courtnall from the Dallas Stars in a trade in April 1995 to reunite him with his older brother, Geoff.

Quinn only coached the younger Courtnall for six games at the end of the 1995–96 regular season and six more in the playoffs after Rick Ley was fired as the Canucks bench boss late in the year.

But Quinn made an impression on Russ Courtnall, not only as a coach but as a general manager. He also had the benefit of his brother Geoff's thoughts. The older Courtnall had played parts of five seasons in Vancouver with Quinn behind the bench.

"There were two hockey men in my career that stood out way above the others—Serge Savard and Pat Quinn," said Courtnall, who played for the Montreal Canadiens when Savard was the GM. "They treated men like men, not boys.

"Pat never forgot what it was like to be a player. He was fair and honest and one of the guys. I told Wayne that he was going to have a bunch of superstars on his team. Guys who were used to playing on the first line, who were going to have to play different roles, maybe on the fourth line. Those guys would listen to Pat. He had a presence. He could get upset. But he had everyone's respect."

Nicholson liked the fact Quinn was a players' coach, a trait he felt necessary in a short-term event like the Olympics.

After two days together in sunny Southern California, Nicholson returned home to Calgary. He didn't wait too long to offer Gretzky the position of executive director of the 2002 Canadian men's Olympic hockey team. Nicholson phoned him the next day and Gretzky climbed aboard. The Great One, however, was a Green One when it came to management. He knew he needed a trusted confidant.

"When I was asked, I was more honoured and more than pleased to do it," Gretzky said. "The only caveat I asked for was to pick Kevin Lowe as my assistant because we were on the same page when it came to all things hockey and what you need to put a team together."

Lowe grew up in Lachute, Quebec, about an hour northwest of Montreal and not far from the Ontario border. His parents owned a local dairy. Eventually, one of the community rinks was named Arena Kevin Lowe–Pierre Page. Page was a longtime NHL head coach.

Lowe enjoyed a Hall of Fame career, bursting on to the scene as a 17-year-old defenceman with the tradition-rich Quebec Remparts, where Guy Lafleur played juniors. In Lowe's third and final season he became the franchise's first English-speaking captain.

Lowe became part of the Edmonton Oilers core leadership group with Gretzky and Mark Messier. The dependable defenceman would win five Stanley Cups in Edmonton and add a sixth alongside Messier with the 1993–94 New York Rangers. The three were together for Canada's title at the 1984 Canada Cup, while Gretzky and Lowe won a bronze medal for Canada at the 1982 World Championship, the spring the Oilers were unexpectedly knocked out in the first round by the Los Angeles Kings.

There was no surprise he made a seamless transition from player to assistant coach to Oilers head coach and then general manager. It also was no surprise the inexperienced Gretzky would lean on Lowe to be his right-hand man in this Olympic endeavour.

"When Wayne called it was very special," Lowe recalled. "I hadn't talked to him for a long time, for no other reason that our playing days had ended, I had kids, he had kids, and we went off in different directions. We were living in Edmonton, he was living in Los Angeles. So I'd say it had been three years since the last time we had talked."

To say Lowe was overwhelmed when he found out why Gretzky called was an understatement. It was a quick and easy decision to join his old friend on this venture.

"It's probably my greatest memory of our friendship, that he would have the trust in me to be a part of this," Lowe said. "First of all, for him to call and make me his first call and secondly to tell [Nicholson] that he would only take the job on the condition I was part of the management team."

Hockey Canada waited until Hockey Hall of Fame week in Toronto to announce Gretzky and Lowe would lead the management team. Pat Quinn was named head coach and his assistants were to be Ken Hitchcock, Jacques Martin, and Wayne Fleming.

It was a busy week. Hockey USA also appointed Herb Brooks as its head coach, hoping he could replicate his successful head coach role in the United States Miracle on Ice golden moment in Lake Placid in 1980, the last time the U.S. had played host to the Winter Games.

Gretzky also would discover he was to be inducted into the Canadian Sports Hall of Fame with the late curler Sandra Schmirler, an Olympic gold medal winner in 1998 and three-time world champion who passed away after a bout with cancer in March 2000.

Fittingly, before players Denis Savard and Joe Mullen were inducted into the Hockey Hall of Fame in November 2000, Bobby Clarke, Paul Henderson, and the rest of the Canadian team from the 1972 Summit Series were honoured with the unveiling of a statue and plaque outside the HHOF building at the corner of Yonge and Front in downtown Toronto.

Gretzky stressed he wouldn't receive a dime for his new role with Hockey Canada and that he was prepared for his place in the hot seat.

"Since 1978, when I played on the world junior team, I loved being part of Team Canada," Gretzky said in the press conference. "I love taking on the responsibility, I love being in that situation. We've put together a really strong staff and we're going to put together a really strong hockey team. I'm looking forward to it.

"There is no question that this is a different era and a different time for Canadian hockey than it was in the 1987 and 1991 Canada Cups and, for that matter, even the 1996 World Cup. The expectation in those days was that nobody could beat the Canadians, and now the thought is, 'Can the Canadians win?' It's changed, but we still have great players and we still have a lot of pride. The Canadian public still demands nothing but gold.

"I love being in that situation. I'm right in the middle of it and I'm looking forward to it. It started today. We put together a good strong staff and we're going to put together a really strong hockey team. At the end of the day, I'll accept the responsibility. I know the Canadian public will accept nothing less than a gold medal."

Canada's chances to win gold received a huge boost a month later. Mario Lemieux had retired from the game after winning his sixth Art Ross Trophy as the 1996–97 NHL scoring champion. He was diagnosed with cancer, Hodgkin's lymphoma to be exact, and announced on January 12, 1993, he would undergo surgery to remove an enlarged lymph node from his neck.

When he retired, four years later, he also was troubled by a wonky back and frustrated with the amount of obstruction and stick work that had crept into the NHL game. He was 32.

Rumblings that Lemieux would end his three-year absence from the game began a week or so after Gretzky was sworn in as Canada's Olympic team executive director. Lemieux made it official with a statement on December 8, 2000. He already had a spot in the Hockey Hall of Fame and he had taken over as the Pittsburgh Penguins' owner. Now, at 35, he was back.

Lemieux made his first public comments two days later, on the same day Gretzky officially became a minority owner of the Phoenix Coyotes. Before Lemieux spoke, the NHL board of governors unanimously approved the sale of the Coyotes from Richard Burke to a group headed by real estate developer Steve Ellman that included Gretzky.

"It's ironic that the day I assume ownership that my partner for many years is going back on the ice," Gretzky said, speaking at the board of governors' meetings in Palm Beach, Florida. "I don't expect him to do anything but play at a level that he's capable of playing at. I think he's going to be a strong force for the Pittsburgh Penguins. He's going to help the NHL both at the box office and image-wise."

Lemieux spoke at the Pittsburgh City Center Marriott a few hours later. He issued a warning to the players around the league, that he wasn't returning to "embarrass himself."

Lemieux also was asked if he wanted to compete for Canada in the Olympics. The Winter Games in Salt Lake City were 14 months away. "If I play next year, I'd love to play in the Olympics—for Canada, obviously," he said. "I was born in Canada and played for them before."

The last line was in reference to the fact that Lemieux, who had lived in Pittsburgh since joining the Penguins in 1984, had Canadian-American dual citizenship.

The first game of his comeback happened to be on December 27 against head coach Pat Quinn and the Toronto Maple Leafs, the beginning of a four-game homestand for the Penguins.

All No. 66 required was 33 seconds to make an impact. He set up linemate Jaromir Jagr for an early goal. Lemieux scored midway through the second period and set up Jiri Hrdina for another four minutes later. All Quinn and his goaltender Curtis Joseph could do was watch in amazement. It was as if Lemieux never left. The Penguins skated off with a 5–0 win.

Gretzky called Lemieux to congratulate him on the opening chapter of his comeback. "It was Wayne Gretzky calling just to congratulate me," Lemieux told reporters after the game. "He might be coming back, too. Let's start a rumour."

The return of the Magnificent One was a gift for Gretzky and Canada. Lemieux piled up 16 goals and 16 assists in 16 games by the time the 2001 NHL All-Star Game rolled around in early February.

Even though his return happened only seven weeks previously, Lemieux was invited to play in the All-Star Game. He certainly was the centre of attention.

The unofficial halfway point to the 2000–01 regular season also marked the first time Nicholson, Gretzky, Lowe, Quinn, and the coaching staff assembled in the same room with Hockey Canada media relations guru Brad Pascall to catch up since the introduction presser back in early November.

Gretzky made a strong impression on the group with his thoughts, his listening skills, his thoroughness, and his yearning of inclusion for each member of the group sitting around the table.

"He established relationships with people he didn't know all that well and as a result established trust," Pascall said.

Added Nicholson, "Wayne knew how to make everyone comfortable. At that All-Star Game, he created an atmosphere of engagement by everyone."

One of the dominant messages from Gretzky was for the entire group to be on the same page.

"We decided as an organization we wanted to be on the same page," said Gretzky, in setting the ground rules about discussing possible players. "I would say to Pat, 'You have to be comfortable if you're up a goal or down a goal to look down the bench to see if this guy or that guy you could be counted on to go on the ice.'

"Can this guy make a difference with our club? Can he be a positive?"

Gretzky already had gone as far as to think about the importance of the support staff, people he was comfortable with and people who would make the players feel at ease. So getting the nod were athletic therapists Ken Lowe (Edmonton) and Jim Ramsay (New York Rangers) as well as equipment managers Barry Stafford (Edmonton) and Pierre Gervais (Montreal). The Great One knew Lowe and Stafford from his days with the Oilers. He knew Ramsay from their three seasons together in New York. Gervais was widely considered one of the best in the business and a top-drawer skate sharpener. He was so popular among the players in 2002 he was asked back for the 2006, 2010, and 2014 Olympic Games.

For an inexperienced hockey executive, Gretzky had the attention of everyone in the room. He sat in the corner of the boardroom table that evening in Denver. To his right was Lowe, followed by Jacques Martin, Bob Nicholson, around to Wayne Fleming, Pat Quinn, Edmonton Oilers media relations person Bill Tuele, who would work with Pascall in Salt Lake City, and Pascall to Gretzky's left.

"I was not surprised and I'm not just saying that because of the way things played out," Lowe said of the first impression Gretzky made on the group. "You won't find another person with the passion for hockey, and that's half the battle when it comes to these things.

"When I played with him, he had a vision of things that was so eye-opening to me. I would ask him, 'How did you come up with that and why were you thinking about that?'"

The Olympics dominated the chatter at the All-Star Game. There was excitement on the ice with the all-Canadian trio of Joe Sakic between Paul Kariya and Theo Fleury enjoying a strong game. But it was Lemieux who continued to be the chief story. He skated on a line with Simon Gagne and Brett Hull as North America defeated the World Team 14–12.

"This is just one of those great stories for the game of hockey," Gretzky said. "Not only is [Lemieux] important for the game of hockey, but he has done something very special for Pittsburgh. He's just an elite athlete."

There were three bits of news from the Canadian side in Denver. Gretzky confirmed no goalies would be among the early roster decisions Canada would announce in late March. He also revealed his group had agreed on a shortlist of between 37 and 40 for the final list of 23 (three goalies, seven defencemen, and 13 forwards). Finally, Gretzky and Nicholson approached Vancouver Canucks director of player personnel Steve Tambellini about adding the same role with the Canadian Olympic team. Tambellini was quick to join this distinguished management group. After all, the Olympic spirit and international hockey ran deep in the Tambellini family.

"There always has been a significance in our family with international hockey starting with my father [Addie] playing for Canada at the 1961 World Championship, and of course, my sons also played for Canada, Jeff at the World Junior Championship and Adam at the Spengler Cup," Tambellini said. "Going into this I felt I had real perspective of the importance of this and the significance to the country.

"I was so excited to be considered to be in the group. The depth of leadership with the group was unbelievable with Wayne Gretzky, Pat Quinn, Bob Nicholson, and the others."

Tambellini had a strong connection with the group, dating back to the 1978 World Junior Championship in Montreal. Tambellini, then 19, was a roommate for the tournament with a 16-year-old Gretzky. Tambellini also worked for Pat Quinn with the Vancouver Canucks for a number of seasons.

As a player, Tambellini won a Stanley Cup as a rookie with the 1979–80 New York Islanders. He also represented Canada at the 1981 World Championship, two decades after his father won the title with Canada, and for the 1988 Canadian Olympic team that peaked too soon with its Izvestia Tournament win in Moscow two months earlier.

The 2002 Canadian Olympic management group had less than six weeks before it was to name the first eight players to the Canadian roster on March 25, 2001. This was something cooked up by the NHL as a marketing tool. The league insisted each of the big six teams from Canada, Finland, Sweden, Russia, Czech Republic, and the United States name a partial roster of between eight and 12 NHL players 11 months before the gold medal final was to be played in Salt Lake City.

United States general manager Craig Patrick, who also was the Penguins GM, filled 10 roster spots with Tony Amonte (Chicago Blackhawks), Brett Hull (Dallas Stars), Mike Modano (Dallas Stars), Doug Weight (Edmonton Oilers), Bill Guerin (Boston Bruins), Chris Drury (Colorado Avalanche), Brian Leetch (New York Rangers), John LeClair (Philadelphia Flyers), Jeremy Roenick (Phoenix Coyotes), and Keith Tkachuk (St. Louis Blues).

On the same day, Gretzky revealed his first eight players. The captain was no surprise. Mario Lemieux received the nod. Rounding out the group were forwards Paul Kariya, Owen Nolan, Joe Sakic, and Steve Yzerman followed by defencemen Rob Blake, Scott Niedermayer, and Chris Pronger.

Seven of the eight players were captains of their teams. Only Blake was not a captain. But he had been the captain in Los Angeles. He was traded to the Colorado Avalanche a month before the first eight Canadian players were named. Sakic, of course, was the long-time Avalanche captain.

Gretzky admitted at the presser that Nolan of the San Jose Sharks edged out MacInnis for the final selection that day, partly because the Blues defenceman was out of action with an eye injury.

"I didn't expect to be one of the earlier picks," Nolan said. "I wanted so badly to be on this team. Being named early took the pressure off. It was a good thing because I got off to a slow start in the fall."

Nolan was an interesting story. He was born in Belfast, Northern Ireland. But his family moved to Thorold, Ontario (near Niagara Falls), when Owen was seven months old. He was the first choice by the Quebec Nordiques in the 1990 NHL draft, the middle of three consecutive first overall selections made by the Nordiques, sandwiched between Mats Sundin in 1989 and Eric Lindros in 1991.

Nolan appeared on his way to being a dominant player, scoring 30 goals in 46 games in the lockout-shortened 1994–95 season. Only Peter Bondra (34) and Jagr (32) scored more that year. The next season, however, stunned Nolan. He was dealt nine games in to San Jose in exchange for defenceman Sandis Ozolinsh. Nolan missed out on a championship as the Avalanche traversed on to win the Stanley Cup in a four-game sweep of the Florida Panthers in June 1996.

Nolan was back on track a few seasons later. In 1999–00, he checked in with 44 goals in 78 games. Only the great Pavel Bure scored more times that season, with 58 goals in 74 outings.

With the playoffs fast approaching, Gretzky, Lowe, and Tambellini kept a watchful eye on the NHL. But for those NHLers out of the playoffs, the 2001 IIHF World Championship was as important.

Fleming was the head coach of Canada's entry in Germany. Hockey Hall of Famer Lanny McDonald was part of the management team. Gretzky enjoyed working with McDonald on this team and, as a result, invited him to Salt Lake City to be part of the Olympics.

At the 2001 World Championship, Canada finished fifth after a 3–0 start that included an impressive 5–1 victory against Russia in its third game. Players like Eric Brewer, Michael Peca—who was injured in the game against Russia—and Ryan Smyth distinguished themselves for a possible spot on the Canadian Olympic team roster.

A few weeks later, the Avalanche won their second Stanley Cup in five years. This was good news considering Sakic and Blake already had been named to the Canadian Olympic team. Adam Foote, Alex Tanguay, and goaltender Patrick Roy were strong candidates.

Following the 2001 NHL draft in South Florida, Quinn, Hitchcock, Martin, Fleming, and video coach Mike Pelino gathered in Banff, Alberta, to discuss systems, opponents, and players. McDonald also stopped by to add his insight from the Worlds.

Fleming was invaluable during these meetings because the Winnipeg, Manitoba, native enjoyed an extensive resume with the international game. After a decade at the helm of the University of Manitoba in Winnipeg, he spent two years with the Canadian national team under Dave King, settling for a silver medal in 1992 at the Albertville Olympics.

He then ventured to Sweden to coach Leksands IF for four years before returning to North America with a pair of two-year assistant coach stints with the New York Islanders and Phoenix Coyotes. Rick Bowness, who became friends with Fleming while in Winnipeg as an assistant coach with the Jets, hired Fleming when Bowness secured his first NHL head coaching position with the Islanders.

"He was the first guy I thought of when I was hired by the Islanders," Bowness said. "We became friends because we had such different coaching backgrounds. I was a player who went right into coaching. He coached Canadian university, in Europe, and with the Canadian national team. He was passionate about the game; his knowledge of the game was something else and he had such an extensive background."

The two were together again as assistants under head coach Bobby Francis in Phoenix. Hitchcock hired Fleming as his assistant in Philadelphia for three years. When Steve Yzerman became the Tampa Bay Lightning general manager, he hired Fleming.

On July 24, 2001, Gretzky and Hockey Canada released a list of 34 players who would be invited to a four-day orientation camp, September 4–7, at the Olympic-sized rink at the Father David Bauer Arena in Calgary:

Goalies (4): Ed Belfour (Dallas), Martin Brodeur (New Jersey), Curtis Joseph (Toronto), Patrick Roy (Colorado)

Defence (12): Rob Blake (Colorado), Eric Brewer (Edmonton), Eric Desjardins (Philadelphia), Adam Foote (Colorado), Ed Jovanovski (Vancouver), Al MacInnis (St. Louis), Richard Matvichuk (Dallas), Derek Morris (Calgary), Scott Niedermayer (New Jersey), Chris Pronger (St. Louis), Wade Redden (Ottawa), Scott Stevens (New Jersey)

Forwards (18): Jason Arnott (New Jersey), Anson Carter (Edmonton), Theo Fleury (New York Rangers), Simon Gagne (Philadelphia), Paul Kariya (Anaheim), Mario Lemieux (Pittsburgh), Eric Lindros (New York Rangers), Brendan Morrow (Dallas), Joe Nieuwendyk (Dallas), Owen Nolan (San Jose), Michael Peca (New York Islanders), Keith Primeau (Philadelphia), Mark Recchi (Philadelphia), Joe Sakic (Colorado), Ryan Smyth (Edmonton), Alex Tanguay (Colorado), Pierre Turgeon (St. Louis), Steve Yzerman (Detroit)

Before camp began, two additions were made. Brendan Shanahan (Detroit) was brought in because Sakic was dealing with a groin issue. Foote had undergone offseason shoulder surgery, so Jay McKee (Buffalo) was added.

There also was a problem with Gagne. It turned out he had suffered a shoulder injury. So Lowe called Jarome Iginla, who was at home in St. Albert, Alberta, just under three hours north on Highway 2 from Calgary.

Iginla was out with family for dinner, a sort of last supper for the summer because he would soon return to Calgary to partake in some informal skates with his Flames teammates. He watched on the television sets around the restaurant highlights of the first day of Canada's orientation camp.

Thankfully, his girlfriend and now his wife, Kara, was home to take Lowe's call. When Kara informed Jarome of the message, he thought it was a prank.

"I thought it was my Flames teammate Todd Simpson," Iginla said. "It sounded like something he would do. I could just see him waiting for me with my equipment over my shoulder, showing up at the Father David Bauer rink and embarrassing myself."

Iginla decided to play it safe. He phoned Lowe. Sure enough, it was true. Iginla's presence in Calgary was required. The experience did wonders for his confidence that season. He scored 52 goals and 98 points—both career highs—to win the 2001–02 Art Ross Trophy and Rocket Richard Trophy as the NHL's top point getter and goal scorer, respectively. Iginla also was voted by his peers the winner of the Lester B. Pearson Award as the most outstanding player.

"For sure, those four days in Calgary helped my confidence," Iginla said. "I was so excited to be there and to walk into the dressing room and see jerseys with the names of Sakic, Yzerman, and Lemieux. It was so neat."

The first indicator Mario Lemieux was the right choice for captain came at the beginning of camp. In an ideal world, Canada and the other countries wanted to hold three or four practices in the days leading up to the Olympic tournament. But NHL commissioner Gary Bettman refused to shut down the regular season any earlier than two days before the first game in Salt Lake City, leaving the players with only one day of practice with their national teams.

Gretzky, as a result, felt it was necessary for Canada to hold a summer camp and schedule three on-ice sessions to go along with team meetings, a golf outing, logistics information sessions, and a team-building dinner downtown with the women's team. He knew most European teams would be holding similar training camps with intrasquad games for charity.

The NHLPA, however, condemned the idea of a summer camp. The players union wanted to limit the camp to 48 hours and also wanted to get away from tryouts. The NHLPA didn't want any on-ice sessions and didn't want to shorten the summer for its constituency.

Therefore, Gretzky set the camp dates as late as possible, in most cases a week or so before training camps were to begin. In the case of Blake, Foote, Roy, Sakic, and Tanguay, a few days before they were scheduled to depart for training camp in Sweden and four exhibition games in Sweden and Finland. That trip was cut short due to the 9/11 attacks in New York; Washington, D.C.; and Shanksville, Pennsylvania.

The ice-time situation was explained to the players in an introductory meeting in Calgary. Then Gretzky, Quinn, the management group, and the coaching staff left the room for a players-only meeting. Lemieux stood up and told the group of players they were going on the ice. A few minutes later, Lemieux walked into Nicholson's office where the managers and coaches had gathered.

"We're going on the ice," Lemieux said.

The on-ice sessions were full of excitement with impressive displays of speed and skill. It was a good beginning for this group with so many possibilities of line combinations and defence pairings. Here were the partnerships on the final days for the two intra-squad teams:

Red Team
Forwards: Fleury-Lindros-Peca, Yzerman-Primeau-Iginla, Smyth-Turgeon-Nolan
Defence: MacInnis-Matvichuk, Jovanovski-Morris, Brewer-Desjardins.

White Team
Forwards: Tanguay-Lemieux-Recchi, Carter-Nieuwendyk-Shanahan, Morrow-Arnott-Kariya
Defence: Stevens-Pronger, Redden-Blake, Niedermayer-McKee

Before the players headed off to their training camps, Nicholson and Hockey Canada hosted a dinner with the management, coaching, and support staffs, as well as the players, at the Chicago Chop House in downtown Calgary. It not only provided an opportunity for the men and women players to get to know each other and share their secrets; it also turned into a real rah-rah evening.

By the time Salt Lake City rolled around, the men were trying to end a 50-year gold medal drought, and the women were pursuing their first gold medal. After winning four straight IIHF World Championships in 1990, 1992, 1994, and 1997, the Canadian women settled for silver with a 3–1 loss to the U.S. in the 1998 Olympic final.

The team dinner in Calgary was such a success some players from both teams spilled across the street that Wednesday evening to Cowboys, a popular nightclub back in Cowtown in those days.

"That dinner was a great night," remembered Canadian star Hayley Wickenheiser, who was inducted into the Hockey Hall of Fame after winning Olympic gold four times, as well as seven world championships. "It was the first time both teams were together before 2002. I remember it being a great party that extended well into the night. The wine was flowing, and I just remember mingling and interacting with several of the men. Nothing in particular comes to mind as far as conversations, but it was a fun night."

The next morning, the men delayed their final skate by an hour in order to shake out the cobwebs. Canadian women's head coach Daniele Sauvageau, a police sergeant in the Royal Canadian Mounted Police, made her players run five kilometres.

"None of us were in any form to be running," Wickenheiser said. "That probably sums up the night."

There was plenty of time to recover before the 2001–02 NHL season commenced on October 3. That's when the tryouts began for the Canadian Olympic team. Eight spots were taken because of the early roster announcement in March. That left three goalies, four defencemen, and eight forwards to be chosen. The deadline was December 22, but the final Canadian selections would be revealed on December 15.

The hockey world, however, suffered a massive blow before the 10-week tryout period began. The 9/11 attacks happened. Los Angeles Kings scouts Garnet "Ace" Bailey and Mark Bavis were on the Boston to Los Angeles United Airlines flight 175 that crashed into the South Tower of the World Trade Center.

Bailey, the Kings' director of pro scouting, was a former Oilers teammate and mentor to Gretzky. The teenager often took advantage of Bailey's cooking skills and ate most of his meals with Ace; his wife, Katherine; and infant son, Todd, when the Oilers were at home. The latter reflected on Bailey, a two-time Stanley Cup champion with the Boston Bruins in the early 1970s, in a tribute published in *Sports Illustrated.*

"I learned a lot of things that first year in Edmonton, and nobody taught me more than Ace Bailey," Gretzky wrote. "I was 17 and he was 30, and he was everything to me—father, teammate, roommate, friend. He taught me about being tough and loyal and about enjoying life. That year we began to build a lasting friendship.

"From day one, Ace took care of me. He told me how to dress and how to act, and I was smart enough to listen. I cared so much about his opinion. He used to brag about me to his friends in Boston. He'd say, 'Wait'll you see this kid play,' and I never wanted to let Ace down."

With a heavy heart, Gretzky refused to let Canada down. The 9/11 attacks also put the future of the Winter Games in Salt Lake City in jeopardy. But time was on the side of the organizers to rebound and make the Olympics secure.

Gretzky, along with Lowe, Tambellini, and Fleming, underwent a hectic travel schedule in the first three months of the NHL season. They held Monday conference calls to update each other on the players and games they had scouted.

The first episode of anxiety happened in a game between the Maple Leafs and Pittsburgh Penguins in Toronto on Saturday, October 27. With Gretzky, Lowe, Tambellini, and Fleming in attendance, Lemieux left the game with a hip injury in the first period. He was on the ice for only eight shifts and six minutes, 30 seconds of ice time. The development overshadowed the victory for Quinn and 23-save shutout for Curtis Joseph.

Lemieux underwent arthroscopic hip surgery two days later in Pittsburgh. He had been bothered by soreness since training camp, when tests revealed there was torn cartilage and a small bone fragment. The Penguins first attempted to treat the ailment with therapy and strengthening exercises. But the hip muscle did not respond to the regimen. Surgery became necessary.

The surgical procedure was expected to keep Lemieux on the sidelines for three weeks to a month. He returned, however, two weeks later. But after three more outings, Lemieux was on the sidelines again—this time for almost two months. He needed healing time. He returned to play in a dozen games before departing for Salt Lake City, collecting a solid five goals and 19 points.

The second scare Gretzky and his management team suffered was on the morning of Wednesday, November 21. Goalie Patrick Roy phoned the Canadian team executive director to say he had no desire to play in Salt Lake City. He told Gretzky that he wanted to employ the Olympic break to rest and prepare for the playoffs.

No worries. Quinn and Gretzky were comfortable with either Brodeur or Joseph. Now came the difficult part—filling out the rest of the roster.

The management and coaching staff assembled in Toronto on Friday, December 14. Ken Hitchcock, whose Dallas Stars were to visit the Phoenix Coyotes the next day, joined the group via telephone.

Sitting around the table at the Westin Harbour Castle hotel that evening were Gretzky, Lowe to his right, followed by Pat Quinn, Bob Nicholson, Jacques Martin, Wayne Fleming, and Steve Tambellini.

There weren't any contentious debates. In fact, the group had time for a steak dinner afterward. Gretzky ran the meeting and, as usual, included everyone's opinion. Ed Belfour beat out Sean Burke for the third goalie position. Eric Lindros snatched the last forward spot over Joe Thornton, Anson Carter, Wayne Primeau, and Alex Tanguay. Ed Jovanovski was given the final blue line position over Wade Redden and Derek Morris.

Gretzky later informed Burke, Redden, Morris, Thornton, Carter, and Tanguay that they were on Canada's six-player taxi squad in case of an injury before Canada's first game in Salt Lake City against Sweden on February 15.

The final Canadian roster looked like this: Belfour, Brodeur, and Joseph in goal; Blake, Brewer, Foote, Jovanovksi, MacInnis, Niedermayer, and Pronger on defence; Fleury, Gagne, Iginla, Kariya, Lemieux, Lindros, Nieuwendyk, Nolan, Peca, Sakic, Shanahan, Smyth, and Yzerman up front. That meant Gretzky had 12 players in Brodeur, Joseph, Blake, Foote, MacInnis, Pronger, Fleury, Lindros, Nieuwendyk, Sakic, Shanahan, and Yzerman returning from the team he played with in Nagano.

Peca, Pronger, Sakic, and Yzerman later were named assistant captains under Lemieux.

Gretzky and the management staff began calling the 15 players added to the mix at noon the next day. The only player that could not be reached was MacInnis. He was coaching his son's game.

Canada's 23-player roster had a combined salary of more than $118 million U.S. But could they deliver the goods in two months?

"This is a great day for hockey in Canada," Gretzky said at the press conference at the Hockey Hall of Fame, in which members of the local Whitby Wildcats novice team wore the sweaters of the players selected for the reveal.

"We truly believe that every player who is on this team deserves to be here and will contribute to hopefully us winning the gold medal."

CHAPTER 3

Curtain-Raiser Reject

Maybe, just maybe, the warning signs were there the summer before that the tournament would not progress without a hitch for Wayne Gretzky and Co. in Salt Lake City.

Hockey Canada wanted to honour its past Olympic glory, not to mention add some capital to the company coffers, with a third sweater that would pay homage to the gold medal conquering Toronto Granites in 1924 at the Winter Games in Chamonix, France. The jerseys were traditional red with shoulder patches that had a version of the Granites logo. The Granites, Allan Cup senior national champions in 1921–22 and 1922–23, destroyed the competition in their trip to the Olympics, outscoring the opposition by a combined score of 132–3.

The Canadian players in 2002 would don this sweater for the first game against Sweden, an outing that turned into a one-sided 5–2 win for Mats Sundin and the Tre Kronor.

"It was such a nice-looking sweater," Steve Tambellini said. "But you never saw that one again after that game"

Maybe the hex was on from the Icelandic community in Winnipeg.

When Hockey Canada unveiled the heritage sweater at a press conference on August 7, 2001, defenceman Scott Niedermayer was on hand to model the new uniform top. To honour the Granites was a well-intentioned venture, but it immediately angered those hockey historians familiar with the Winnipeg Falcons' plight four years earlier than the Granites' victory.

Hockey Canada had incorrectly determined the Granites were Canada's first gold medal victors at the Olympics. The Falcons won gold at the 1920 Summer Games in Antwerp, Belgium. It was the first time the hockey competition had been introduced at the Olympics and because it was contested at the Summer Games, Hockey Canada dignitaries felt this competition was a demonstration and, therefore, that the Granites were the first team to win hockey gold.

Well, the dismissal of the Falcons' accomplishment caused quite the firestorm in Winnipeg, especially with those who knew about the team's story and their 12–1 victory against Sweden in the 1920 final. The Falcons were a team of second-generation Icelandic Canadians, and they left behind a proud legacy in Manitoba because of their golden moment.

Maybe Hockey Canada should have consulted Gretzky before the decision was made to honour the Granites over the Falcons. He stumbled upon the folklore of the Falcons' famed captain Frank Fredrickson while house-hunting with his wife, Janet, in St. Louis after Gretzky was traded to the Blues in February 1996.

Janet and Wayne were touring a home when Wayne noticed a room with all sorts of hockey photos. It turns out the house was owned by Dr. John Fredrickson, the son of the famous Falcons centre.

Gretzky was curious and inquired about the hockey pictures. He learned all about Fredrickson, a lawyer. Gretzky heard about the Falcons' upset of the University of Toronto to capture the 1920 Allan Cup national senior championship a few months before the Summer Olympics. After winning gold in Antwerp, Fredrickson joined the Victoria Aristocrats and later the Victoria Cougars, a club he celebrated a Stanley Cup championship with in 1924–25. After stops in

Detroit, Boston, Pittsburgh, and Detroit again, Fredrickson coached at Princeton University. He was inducted into the Hockey Hall of Fame in 1958.

Hockey Canada, meanwhile, attempted to rectify the Falcons flop by placing decals on the Canadian players' helmets in Salt Lake City to commemorate the 1920 Olympians. But the Falcons finally received their rightful reverence at the beginning of the 2004 World Cup of Hockey. With many of these same Canadian players from the 2002 Olympics, like Mario Lemieux, Joe Sakic, Scott Niedermayer, Adam Foote, and Martin Brodeur, Canada wore replica Falcons yellow and black sweaters in their tournament-opening 2–1 win at the Bell Centre in Montreal.

Sidney Crosby and the Canadian world junior team also donned the replica Falcons sweater for an exhibition game against Finland in Winnipeg in December 2004 before the world junior was to begin two hours south in Grand Forks, North Dakota.

Credit Hockey Canada with making things right with the Icelandic-Canadian community. When it came time to plan a possible victory celebration in the event of a Canadian win, Hockey Canada needed a venue to house the players, coaches, managers, support staff, family members, and VIPs, just in case. The Iceland Olympic Committee had set up the Icelandic House as its home base at the Tomax Building in downtown Salt Lake City. Through connections with friends made from the Canadian-Icelandic community in Winnipeg over the Falcons miscue, Hockey Canada procured possession of the Icelandic House for their gold medal party.

That particular party at the Icelandic House on the Sunday evening after the gold medal game, and the blowout that ensued across Canada, was long overdue. What was a bountiful start to the 1990s for Canadian hockey hit a wall at the end of the decade and the early part of the turn of the century. The Canadian women had gone a perfect seven-for-seven in the IIHF World Women's Championships contested between 1990 and 2001, but they arrived in Salt Lake City with something to prove after their disheartening 3–1 loss to the rival United States in the final in 1998 at the Nagano Olympics.

On the men's side, the Canadian junior program was on a roll for most of the 1990s, winning back-to-back titles in 1990 and 1991 and following up with five in a row between 1993 and 1997. Several 2002 Olympians tasted part of the Canadian junior success, including Eric Lindros, Scott Niedermayer, Paul Kariya, Chris Pronger, Michael Peca, Ryan Smyth, and Jarome Iginla.

But even the Canadian junior program got stuck in the mud after 1997. It didn't win gold again until the Darryl Sutter–coached, Sidney Crosby–led edition pulled the program out of its doldrums in 2005 with a championship in Grand Forks.

Before the NHL decided to join the Olympic party, the Canadian national team enjoyed success under head coach Dave King in 1992 and his successor, Tom Renney, in 1994 with a pair of silver medal showings. The 1992 team in Albertville featured Lindros, while a 19-year-old Kariya burst onto the scene two years later. He scored the overtime winner against the Czechs in a 3–2 victory in the quarterfinals. He set up another in Canada's 5–3 win against Finland in the semifinals and another in the gold medal final, a 3–2 shootout loss to Peter Forsberg and Sweden.

"Having that experience in 1994 and coming within a shootout of winning gold was helpful in 2002," Kariya said. "But in many ways the experience was so different from 1994. We weren't expected to win in 1994 like we were in 2002. The expectations were so different. The pressure was different. But that doesn't mean we didn't believe we could win in 1994, so we did have that internal pressure."

The internal pressure mounted for Canada each spring at the world championship since Canada decided to return to the annual tournament in 1977 with a roster full of NHL players who were eliminated from the playoffs. Canada finished fourth in its return, won a bronze the following year, and duplicated the third-place finish in 1982 and 1983.

But as the losses piled up at the world championship, Canadian Hockey now had another troublesome championship-less streak that had elapsed far too long. The last time Canada had won the world title was back in 1961, when the Trail Smoke Eaters were triumphant. Steve Tambellini's father, Addie, was a key performer on the Trail team.

There were high hopes for Canada in 1985 when a couple of hotshot teenagers in Mario Lemieux and Steve Yzerman decided to play for their country at the world championship tournament in Prague. Lemieux was coming off his rookie season with the Pittsburgh Penguins. Yzerman had just completed his second year with the Detroit Red Wings.

Lemieux's tournament didn't start out well. He asked to fly back to Quebec, citing homesickness. But after sitting out an early game, he picked up his play to lead Canada offensively with four goals and 10 points in nine outings. Yzerman wasn't far behind with three goals and seven points in 10 games.

Canada advanced to the final round-robin against then Czechoslovakia, Russia, and the United States. A 3–2 victory over the U.S. followed by a morale-boosting 3–1 win against Russia put Canada in the gold medal final against the host country. Canada was feeling good about itself because Russia had hammered Canada 9–1 in the preliminary round.

In the final, the Czechs went ahead 3–2 on a shorthanded goal from Jiri Sejba, who grew up in Pardubice with future Canada-beater Dominik Hasek. Sejba would make it 4–2 on a goal the Canadians felt was offside. Canada pulled to within 4–3 but would lose 5–3 on an empty netter. There would be another bronze for Canada in 1986 and losses in the gold medal final to the Soviet Union in 1989 and to Sweden in 1991.

The gold-less streak at the world championship had stretched to 32 years after Russia, Sweden, and the Czechs finished one, two, three, respectively, in Munich in 1992. Canada claimed fourth after a 7–4 defeat to the Russians in the semifinals and 5–1 loss to the Czechs in the bronze medal match. Would the tide turn for Canada the following spring in Milan, Italy, three months after the heart-breaking shootout at the Lillehammer Olympics?

An imposing group of Canadians arrived in Italy for coach George Kingston's side. Again, there was a thread to the 2002 Olympic team with Kariya, Sakic, Blake, and Brendan Shanahan. Led by the inspired play of Kariya, Canada skated through the preliminary round with a 5–0 record, outscoring the host Italian team, Austria, Germany, Great Britain, and Russia by a combined score of 24–7.

Shayne Corson scored the late game-winner for a 3–2 victory in a close quarterfinal match against the Czechs. Luc Robitaille scored a hat trick and Bill Ranford earned a shutout in a 6–0 win against Sweden in the semifinals to avenge the loss in the Olympic final a few months earlier. This put Canada into the finals against a strong team from Finland, which dismantled the United States 8–0 in the semifinals.

The tight-checking final progressed to the third period without a goal. Finland grabbed a 1–0 advantage 6:51 into the third frame, but Rod Brind'Amour pulled Canada even with a power-play goal with less than five minutes remaining in regulation. The game evolved to overtime, then a shootout, then an extra shootout round. Robitaille closed the deal for Canada.

"It was such a satisfying win because it not only erased some of the disappointment from the loss to Sweden in Lillehammer," said Kariya, who as a 19-year-old had yet to have played a game in the NHL but led Canada with five goals and 12 points in eight outings. "We ended a long winless streak that Canadian hockey went through. It wasn't quite the 50 years between the gold medals in the Olympics, but ending the world championship drought at 33 years was a big deal."

Canada won another world championship in Helsinki, Finland, three years later. This was sort of a trial run for the 1998 Olympic Games. Like the 1998 team, Bobby Clarke, Bob Gainey, and Pierre Gauthier comprised the management team for Canada in 1997. Andy Murray was the head coach in 1997 and a big part of Marc Crawford's staff a year later in Nagano. There were five players who performed for both teams in Blake, Pronger, Keith Primeau, Mark Recchi, and Rob Zamuner. Canada scored only 13 goals in its six medal-round games, a puny offensive total that should have set off alarm bells for Nagano.

Still, the 1997 World Championship team, which also included future 2002 Olympians Iginla and Owen Nolan, was the lone bright spot for Canadian men's hockey at the end of the decade and right up until Salt Lake City.

The uneasiness with the direction of the way the game was going in Canada began to jack up in the fall of 1996. The Canada Cup morphed into the World Cup of Hockey in 1996. It had been Canada's domain. Darryl Sittler provided the heroics with the overtime goal against the Czechs in the inaugural best-on-best tournament in 1976, but it was

Bobby Orr's last brilliant stand before his troublesome knees forced him out of the game for good.

Wayne Gretzky and Canada fell victim to the Soviet Union in the 1981 Canada Cup with a humiliating 8–1 loss in the final. The Big Red Machine was plenty motivated after it had been upset by the young United States squad in the 1980 Olympics, a master stroke victory that inspired the movie *Miracle*, starring Kurt Russell as U.S. coach Herb Brooks.

With Gretzky leading the way, it was all Canada in the next three Canada Cups in 1984, 1987, and 1991. The middle victory produced a goal as famous as Paul Henderson's late-minute Summit Series clincher in 1972. Fifteen years later, Gretzky to Lemieux with 86 seconds remaining for a 6–5 win against Russia in the finale was one of those "where were you" moments.

The 1987 Canadian team rivalled the 2002 Olympic team for pure star power with 12 eventual Hockey Hall of Famers to 14 in 2002.

Canada, however, lost the best-of-three final to the United States in 1996. While the apologists for Canadian hockey pleaded for calm because Canada was defeated by a superior goaltending effort from tournament MVP Mike Richter, there were calls to revamp the Canadian hockey system.

In 1996, Canada squeezed by Sweden 3–2 thanks to Theo Fleury's winner in double overtime. The United States handled Russia 5–2 in the other semifinal to set up a best-of-three final between the North American rivals to begin in Philadelphia with the remaining games in Montreal.

Canada continued its overtime magic in the first opener with a 4–3 victory when Yzerman scored late in the first extra period. But the U.S. rebounded with a strong 5–2 win in Game 2. John LeClair, a former Montreal Canadiens forward, scored twice in the win, and Richter made 35 stops.

In the finale, Canada enjoyed a strong opening period, but Richter kept his team even at 1–1. Adam Foote drifted a long shot to push Canada in front with 7:01 remaining in the third period to give Canada hope of keeping its international hockey crown. But Brett Hull deflected a Brian Leetch shot to tie things up four minutes later for his second of the game. The Canadian players were hot, claiming Hull changed the direction of Leetch's drive with a high stick. But after a video review, the goal was allowed to stand. The tying goal unnerved Canada. Tony Amonte put the Americans ahead 43 seconds later from in close. Goals from Derian Hatcher and Canadian-born dual citizen Adam Deadmarsh in the last minute ended the drama in the deciding game to give the U.S. a 5–2 win.

This defeat, coupled by Canada's disappointing loss to the Czech Republic in the semifinals at the 1998 Olympics, had the critics of Canada's game licking their chops. The result was Hockey Canada organizing the Open Ice Hockey summit held in Toronto in August 1999. Gretzky was involved in the three days of workshops, debate, and speeches.

Eleven recommendations were made as a result of the summit, everything from hiring salaried mentors or master coaches for each minor hockey organization to developing a mental skills component to altering the practice to game ratio in favour of more practices to developing more sports schools. Former players like Steve Larmer blamed the use of systems for players at an early age. Gretzky agreed and urged the importance of outdoor pickup games at a young age.

"When we were younger, guys like [Bobby] Orr and [Jean] Beliveau used to play on frozen ponds and rivers and learn to be creative and a little more imaginative by just handling the puck," Gretzky said. "We seem to be a little more structured today. At nine years old I don't think a kid needs to learn to play a trap."

Summit or no summit, by the time the Salt Lake City Olympics rolled around there was an immense amount of pressure on the men's side of Canadian hockey. There were the 1996 World Cup and 1998 Olympic disappointments. The world junior program struggled with only two silver medals in five tournaments between 1998 and 2002. Since Pronger and his peeps won the 1997 World title, Canada finished sixth in 1998, fourth in 1999 and 2000, and fifth in 2001.

The 2001 result was especially difficult to take because it was the United States who eliminated Canada in the quarterfinals thanks to an overtime goal from Darby Hendrickson.

Even the Canadian team at the Spengler Cup experienced a mini drought. The Spengler Cup is a tournament contested between Christmas and New Year's Day in Davos, Switzerland. Canada puts together an annual entry that mostly consists of Canadians playing pro in Europe. After winning four in a row between 1995 and 1998, Canada failed to win again at the prestigious tournament until nine months after Sakic and his teammates triumphed in Salt Lake City.

"The 50-year drought was out there in the media and because Wayne and Kevin were Edmonton guys who had so much success there, the whole Edmonton Mercurys story was played up, too," Tambellini said. "But this was a real low point in Canadian hockey, particularly because of what happened in 1996 [at the World Cup of Hockey] and the 1998 [Olympics]. It became a significant talking point in the months and weeks leading into Salt Lake City."

Canada had concerns one month out from the first game against Sweden in Salt Lake City. Captain Mario Lemieux was about to return after two months off due to his hip issues. Al MacInnis was slated to miss two weeks with back problems, and Adam Foote was out with a knee injury.

On top of these matters, Eric Lindros had returned to action from injury but had scored only once in seven games since taking time off with a concussion. Simon Gagne had yet to find his form after a layoff because of a shoulder injury.

All eyes were on Lemieux in mid-January. The Magnificent One was slated to return on Saturday, January 12, just 34 days before Canada was to open the men's Olympic tournament against Sweden. Lemieux's Penguins were defeated 4–1 against the St. Louis Blues in his return. But he was pleased with his progress.

"The way I'm skating now, the way I feel every day, in another month I will be at the top of my game hopefully and will try to help Team Canada bring home a gold medal," he said a couple days after the game against the Blues.

Lemieux's next game was in Vancouver, and he shared his Olympic excitement with reporters prior to Pittsburgh's 5–2 defeat, in which Lemieux scored his first goal since October 23.

"I missed the game for three and a half years," Lemieux said. "To have a chance to come back and be successful, you appreciate things a little more. Another month and I'll be on top of my game and help Team Canada try to win a gold medal. I'm really looking forward to it.

"It would be a great accomplishment just to be part of Team Canada and have a chance to win a gold medal at age 36. It would be right up there with my two Stanley Cups. The '87 Canada Cup was very special. The Olympics would be right up there."

Lemieux did gather steam. Beginning in Vancouver, he collected points in seven of eight games, including five goals and 18 points. He also felt spry enough to play in the All-Star Game in Los Angeles, scoring a goal and playing on a line with Paul Kariya and Joe Sakic.

It was Lemieux's 13 career goal in All-Star Games, tying a record set by Wayne Gretzky.

At the All-Star Game, Gretzky and the management staff assembled with Pat Quinn and the coaching contingent to go over game strategies and discuss contingency plans if one or more of these injuries were to knock a Canadian player out of the Olympic Games.

Ken Hitchcock arrived in Los Angeles with more free time than expected. The Dallas Stars had fired their coach, who steered the Stars to the 1998–99 Stanley Cup title, the previous weekend. The career coach was more than willing to jump in to aid Wayne Fleming with video analysis and devising schemes to combat the opposition.

Canadian Olympians Rob Blake, Jarome Iginla, Ed Jovanovski, Kariya, Owen Nolan, Chris Pronger, Sakic, and Brendan Shanahan also were in Los Angeles to play in the All-Star Game. Lindros had been named to the North American team but opted out with a knee injury.

Gretzky and the Canadian officials were confident Lindros would be 100 per cent healthy by the time he would depart for Salt Lake City. Detroit Red Wings captain Steve Yzerman was another matter.

The Great One arrived in Salt Lake City on Saturday, February 9, and held his first press conference to provide an update on his injured players. There were still five nights of action in the NHL, including that evening, before the league shut down for the Olympics. Gretzky reported that Lindros was fine, as was Owen Nolan, who was dealing with a sore back. Al MacInnis was also expected to play, despite a sore ankle he suffered after blocking a shot and after he had healed from his back woes.

Now the concern was Paul Kariya, who required four stitches on his baby finger to repair a gash caused when he was hit with a shot in practice. But Kariya didn't miss any time. Yzerman remained the only player in doubt. Gretzky revealed that Joe Thornton would replace Yzerman if the veteran forward couldn't perform.

At his pre-tournament press conference that day, Gretzky discussed everything from the Russians and Swedes to his experience as Canada's executive director to his team's bid to end the 50-year drought to the difference between winning a Stanley Cup and Olympic gold.

"I've never had the feeling of a gold medal yet," Gretzky remarked. "But I'm hoping that changes.

"You can't measure chemistry and heart, but that's what it takes to win championships. But we're ready for the big ice surface. This is as fast as any team you've seen play for Canada. We like where we're at.

"This has been a great, great experience for me, but a lot of work. The Olympics are something that comes around only once every four years. We're proud of our game in Canada. It's a privilege to be part of this."

Yzerman underwent arthroscopic right knee surgery to have cartilage removed on January 28. He had been bothered by the ailment for a few weeks, but after back-to-back outings on January 25–26 that resulted in more soreness, surgery was decided as the course of action. He began skating 10 days after the procedure and set games in Montreal and Minnesota on February 11 and 13, respectively, to test his knee and make a decision on whether to compete for Canada in the Olympics.

"If there's a problem with the knee, I won't be going," said Yzerman in a conference call with reporters. "Having said that, I fully expect to be fine. But there are other guys just as good who are healthy."

Yzerman was healthy enough to play. Detroit won both games. He assisted on both the Red Wings' goals in their 2–0 victory against the Wild. Yzerman's mind was at ease as he and Shanahan made their way to Salt Lake City the morning after Detroit's game in Minnesota.

Canada had 13 of its 23 players competing on the final evening before the Olympic break was to begin. That meant Yzerman, Shanahan, Pronger, MacInnis, Sakic, Foote, Blake, Lindros, Fleury, Nieuwendyk, Belfour, Iginla, and Kariya would be flying to Salt Lake City on the morning of Thursday, February 14. Iginla, Pronger, and MacInnis were all coming off back-to-back situations with games on February 12–13.

Brodeur, Niedermayer, Lemieux, Peca, Nolan, Gagne, Smyth, Brewer, and Jovanovski saw their final NHL action before the Olympic break on the 12th, while Joseph watched from the bench for his team's final pre-break outing. Canada had only one practice to prepare for Sweden. As the players convened in Salt Lake City from across North America, that first of 11 days together proved to be a hectic one.

"It was a crazy day," Foote said. "By the time we had a tour of the Olympic Village, a practice that was full tilt, media responsibilities, meetings, and video sessions, we were exhausted."

After becoming settled in the Olympic Village, located near downtown Salt Lake City on the University of Utah campus, the Canadian players boarded a bus bound for the E Center. They had to dress at the E Center and get back on the bus for a 15-minute drive to the practice rink, the Accord Ice Center.

Canadian team media relations director Brad Pascall had been in Salt Lake City in time to march in the opening ceremony with video coach Mike Pelino and Hockey Canada executive Johnny Misley. Pascall was much more than the team's media relations guru. He was a jack of all trades, a close confidant of Gretzky's.

Pascall was good enough to be a fifth-round selection of the Buffalo Sabres in 1990. The Coquitlam, British Columbia, native played four years on the blue line at the University of North Dakota. It was no surprise that after his tenure in the Hockey Canada front office he became an assistant general manager with the Calgary Flames. He learned plenty during his time with Gretzky before and during the 2002 Olympics.

"There was a good marriage between the management team, the coaching staff, and Hockey Canada, and that was Wayne," Pascall said. "He had a good rapport with the players, and he established relationships with people he didn't know in order to establish a level of trust."

With the 2002 Olympics in Salt Lake City being the biggest sporting event since the 9/11 attacks, security was at a heightened level. Any visitor to the Winter Games was immediately struck by the heavy police presence and the Black Hawk helicopters that hovered over the city, as well as being constantly subjected to pocket-emptying magnetometer checks when they entered official venues.

Pascall did his due diligence. He mapped out the route from the E Center to the practice rink and all the security check points as a precaution before the day all the players arrived in town.

"The practice rink was 15 minutes away, but with traffic and security we budgeted 30 minutes, and we were still 15 minutes late," recalled Pascall, who added that the luggage compartments under each bus were welded shut so these nooks could not be tampered with. At the security checks, police would hold mirrors at the end of a pole to look underneath the vehicles.

When the Canadians finally hit the ice for their skate, the first player on was Brendan Shanahan. The fact that he was the last shooter for Canada in the shootout loss to Dominik Hasek in the semifinals four years earlier was not lost on the interested observers in the stands, including Gretzky.

Hockey nuts love line combinations and defence pairings. After two years of watching Gretzky build this Canadian team, there was massive interest to see what Quinn, Hitchcock, Jacques Martin, and Fleming came up with. They kept the All-Star Game trio of Lemieux between Sakic and Kariya together. Yzerman was with his Detroit teammate Shanahan and sniper Iginla. Lindros centred Smyth and Nolan, while Peca was between Nieuwendyk and Fleury.

The pairings on the blue line had Foote and Blake together. This tandem was stellar in Nagano. They weren't on together for a goal against. Pronger was alongside Niedermayer, while the oldest player in MacInnis, 38, was with 22-year-old Brewer. Only Gagne, at 21, was younger among the Canadians.

Quinn already stated he planned to dress a roster of 12 forwards and six d-men, like in the NHL, instead of the 20 skaters the international game allows. That meant it appeared Jovanovski and Gagne would not dress for the first game. Quinn also confirmed that Joseph would start in goal with Brodeur seeing action in either Game 2 against Germany or the final preliminary round game against the Czech Republic.

"We have five days and three games to shortcut the team building concept," Quinn said. "We don't have to win any of these games, but we intend to win them all."

This became Quinn's mantra in the preliminary round, and in hindsight, became a phrase the Canadian players needed to believe in if they wanted to end the five-decade dry spell.

"If you can't play under pressure, maybe you should watch on TV," said Lemieux in his final message to reporters on the eve of the tournament.

The weary Canadians went to bed with some inspiration provided from Canadian speed skater Catriona Le May Doan on Thursday evening. She won the country's first gold medal of the Salt Lake City Games, successfully defending her 500-metre Olympic championship from Nagano on Valentine's Day with her husband, Bart, in the stands.

After her emotional win, she grabbed her husband's cowboy hat for her victory lap. The Saskatoon, Saskatchewan, athlete performed under stupendous pressure following a disastrous fall by her speedskating teammate, Jeremy Wotherspoon. He was a favourite in the men's 500-metre but stumbled and wiped out at the start of his race to finish 13th.

Le May Doan helped put the entire Canadian Olympic team on track. The next morning, as Lemieux and the Canadian men's hockey team prepared for its late afternoon game against Sweden, good vibrations reverberated throughout the rest of the Canadian contingent.

First, Beckie Scott made history. The determined athlete from Vermilion, Alberta, became the first North American woman to win an Olympic medal in cross-country skiing.

Competing out at Soldier Hollow, the furthest venue at 85 kilometres southeast from downtown Salt Lake City, Scott initially finished third in the five-kilometre pursuit for a bronze medal. But that bronze eventually turned into gold when first-place finisher Olga Danilova from Russia and her fellow countrywoman Larissa Lazutina, who placed second, were disqualified for using the performance-enhancing drug darbepoetin.

Scott always had been outspoken about the suspected drug use in her sport. She was suspicious of the two Russians who finished ahead of her before the medal presentation.

"I can stand on the podium and wear my medal and know that I did it," Scott told the *Edmonton Sun*. "I was successful, and I was clean. I felt I didn't compete against an entirely clean field."

It took almost two and a half years for Scott to officially be awarded her coveted gold medal. It was worth the wait. Canadian figure skaters Jamie Sale and David Pelletier only had to wait five days for their judging injustice to be rectified.

At the same time word filtered to the Olympic broadcast and media building about Scott's brilliant performance on Friday morning, a press conference was about to begin to award Sale and Pelletier gold medals in the pairs competition after a judging scandal placed them in second.

The final session of the pairs competition took place on Monday evening. The Russian pair, Elena Berezhnaya and Anton Sikharulidze, skated skillfully. They scored well in the artistic category, but their technical performance was severely hindered by a slip from Sikharulidze on a landing.

Sale and Pelletier wowed the audience with a near-flawless performance. After their routine, the crowd chanted "six, six," in reference to a perfect score in figure skating. But after the judges' scores were added up, the Russians were awarded gold. The fans greeted the news with whistles and jeers.

Over the next three days, public outrage mounted. But Ottavio Cinquanta, the head of the International Skating Union, and his organization stumbled along in its investigation. It wasn't until Jacques Rogge, the new International Olympic Committee president, became involved that a reversal was possible.

The French judge, Marie-Reine Le Gougne, admitted to misconduct and subsequently was suspended. She confessed that she was pressured to vote in favour of the Russians. But the inquiry into the controversy never concluded where the pressure came from.

The *Globe and Mail* reported in its Friday morning edition that there was a strong possibility that Sale and Pelletier would be awarded gold medals after all. As the Canadian duo looked on from the Olympic Village, Rogge confirmed the outcome on television. A media conference with a packed room full of reporters was held later that morning.

"It was amazing, it was unbelievable," Sale said as she described her emotions. "A really big surprise for us."

There was no French judge to blame a few hours later in Canada's opener against Sweden. With Sale and Pelletier in the crowd, Canada was soundly beaten by Mats Sundin and Sweden 5–2.

Three shifts into the game at the E Center, Sale, Pelletier and Le May Doan and the rest of the Canadian fans were on their feet, celebrating an early goal from Rob Blake. Canada made it look easy. Michael Peca slid a perfect pass into the middle and Blake stepped into a hard slapper that whistled its way past Sweden goalie Tommy Salo, a teammate in Edmonton with Canadian forward Ryan Smyth and defenceman Eric Brewer.

"I'm glad we got trounced and lost early," Blake said. "If there is a right time to lose, it's better to lose early and not late. It probably was the best thing that could have happened to us, just to realize how good these other teams were and how different the styles were.

"There were a lot of distractions early on. But we knew we had a good team, and it was going to get better."

It went from good to worse after Blake's tournament-opening goal. Other than a late goal from Brewer, there was little to cheer for on the Canadian side in this curtain-raiser.

By the time the game was 20 minutes old, things were tied 1–1. By the time the game hit its second intermission, Sweden enjoyed a 5–1 lead. Brewer's goal did little to stem the disappointment and anxiety over the 5–2 loss.

Lindros had a possible third goal wiped out 25 seconds later in the third period because of goaltender interference. Niedermayer and Nieuwendyk both rattled shots off the post, but these near-misses and a much better final 20 minutes didn't hide Canada's opening-night flop.

The Sweden line of Sundin between Daniel Alfredsson and Ulf Dahlen was outstanding. Sundin scored twice on his Toronto Maple Leafs teammate, Joseph, while Dahlen added a power-play marker for Sweden's fifth and final goal with 4:02 remaining in the second period. Meanwhile, Lemieux appeared sluggish and still bothered by his wonky hip. His linemates, Kariya and Sakic, did little to push Lemieux on the right track.

The Swedes' "Torpedo" system gave Canada fits. It called for long stretch or breakaway passes to take advantage of the no-centre-line regulation in the international game that eliminates two-line offside passes (a rule that was adopted by the NHL in 2005). The Tre Kronor Torpedo also incorporated an aggressive 2-1-1 forechecking system that can give the opposition difficulty if it's not on its game, like the Canadians on this day.

Sweden head coach Hardy Nilsson corrected reporters following the game, saying that he no longer called his system the Torpedo, but rather "big ice hockey."

Quinn wanted his group to function together as five-player units with swift short passes to navigate their way up the ice. Defensively, he wanted to keep the opposition to the outside. He wanted to keep the gap between the forwards and defence tight and he wanted to establish an aggressive forecheck. But not one iota of this game plan was evident in the second period when Sweden exploded for four goals.

"I still remember in the dressing room after the first period thinking about their Torpedo, 'Hey, why don't we try that,' it looks like fun the way they stretched out their game," Sakic said. "It didn't work out that well."

Canada appeared out of sync. Nothing was crisp about its game; even the line changes were lethargic.

"I actually thought we had a good first period," Shanahan said. "But in the dressing room there was a lot of talk about how much we could run out of position, and we needed to have discipline. But for some reason we ignored that. We were too passive, and they put on a clinic in that second period.

"It was a real come-down-to-earth moment for us. It helped us as players, and it helped the coaching staff reset. We didn't have a humility problem, but the adversity we faced in the first game was a wake-up call to get our act together."

Canadian assistant coach Jacques Martin had an interesting theory on why his players didn't have their act together against Sweden. He saw it time and time again in the spring when the playoffs rolled around. Players upped their focus and intensity when the stakes were elevated. Canada didn't have its intensity and focus up in the required stratosphere for the 10-day Olympic tournament. The Canadians had to find their playoff groove.

"We were still stuck in mid-season form," Martin said. "We weren't in playoff intensity mode yet."

Foote didn't necessarily agree with Martin's assessment. The dependable defenceman believes the Canadians had a whirlwind two days in traveling to Salt Lake City and practicing and never caught their collective breath before clashing with Sweden.

"It's interesting to hear all these different opinions," Foote said. "We were dead tired. Remember, after flying in and practicing there was a long meeting that night. It was a long, long day for us. Sweden was a good team and they caught us off guard with their play through the neutral zone.

"We learned to play between the dots, especially defensively. If you were going to venture outside the dots you either had to stop them or have support. This area improved for us as the tournament went on."

As examples of the lack of focus and intensity on the Canadian side, Martin cited the length of the shifts, and too many times Sweden caught Canada with ill-timed line changes.

"We didn't play hard enough and we weren't committed enough," Martin said. "But these were all areas that could be fixed within our group."

There was no doubt the Swedes were considered a medal contender. But they were without one of their better players in injured forward Peter Forsberg. Oddsmakers in Las Vegas had installed Canada as the 8–5 favourites, followed by Russia at 2–1 and the Czech Republic and United States at 5–2. Sweden was listed at 15–1.

While media experts and the fans were quick to criticize and condemn the Canadians, there was calm inside the dressing room.

"The beauty of the Olympics is that you have two more games until the big tournament starts," Lemieux said. "It gives us a chance to adjust, get the guys together."

CHAPTER 4

GERMAN CAPER

Few words were spoken during the 45-minute ride back from Provo to Salt Lake City on Sunday evening, two days after Canada's deflating 5–2 loss to Sweden in the tournament opener. Sitting in the vehicle were Wayne Gretzky, Bob Nicholson, Kevin Lowe, Steve Tambellini, Lanny McDonald, and Brad Pascall.

The Canadians had a day to practice and shake off the disappointment of the curtain-raising clunker before taking on Germany in Canada's only game at the Peaks Ice Arena in Provo. The Canadians squeezed out a 3–2 win against the Germans, but they failed to wipe out the trepidation caused by their showing in the opener.

"It was a very quiet ride home," Nicholson recalled. "Very quiet. Not much had to be said."

What was worse, losing to a medal contender like Sweden or escaping with a narrow victory to one of the weaker countries like Germany?

"I'd throw out the game against Sweden because it was the first game," Canadian defenceman Adam Foote said. "We never played well against Germany. It's just the way it is."

Foote was right. The tight-checking Germans enjoyed a few benchmark days against Canada in international hockey, especially at the 1996 IIHF World Championship in Vienna, Austria, when Martin Brodeur, Paul Kariya, and the favoured Canadian side were shocked 5–1 by the Germans in the preliminary round.

In Provo, the Germans hung back, content to play defence. They often strung five players on their blue line, daring the Canadians to break through.

"I don't think the situation was too dire after the Germany game," Chris Pronger said. "They hung back and made life difficult. We still won. But we were nowhere near where we wanted to be."

What added to the anxiety was a major development at practice on Saturday, the day before the German game. It was evident captain Mario Lemieux wasn't 100 per cent. The hip issues he had been dealing with had returned. He was on the ice for practice, but for the most part he didn't participate in many drills and seemed satisfied to skate along the boards by himself. He wasn't involved in the new line combinations, too, leading to speculation that he wouldn't play against Germany.

Gretzky stated after practice that Lemieux would decide on his own if he wanted to play against Germany or if he felt the prudent option was to save himself for the following day against Dominik Hasek and the Czechs. Before the Olympics, Lemieux vowed to play in each of Canada's six games in the 10-day tournament. He performed in back-to-back games in the NHL 2001–02 regular season only twice in late October and again in mid-November. But he avoided outings on successive nights when he returned after his two-month layoff in January.

Lemieux was sluggish in the opener. Everyone noticed. Even Curt "Curre" Lundmark, Sweden's 1994 Olympic head coach in the shootout gold medal win against Canada, said during the Swedish broadcast that "Lemieux is skating like an old tractor."

In the end, Lemieux watched from the stands in Provo. He wasn't the only lineup change head coach Pat Quinn made. As mentioned, Quinn initially planned to dress an NHL-type model of 12 forwards and six defencemen. But he scrapped that idea for the rest of the tournament with a full international-style complement of seven d-men and 13 forwards. That meant Ryan Smyth and Ed Jovanovski, the two players who sat out the first game against Sweden, suited up against Germany.

With Lemieux out, the new line combinations the coaching staff came up with were Joe Sakic between Jarome Iginla and Simon Gagne, a unit that immediately paid dividends and would continue its prowess for the rest of the tournament. Lindros centred Kariya and Owen Nolan. Joe Nieuwendyk skated with Steve Yzerman and Smyth, while Michael Peca played between Theo Fleury and Brendan Shanahan. On defence, Al MacInnis and Chris Pronger stayed together. Eric Brewer and Rob Blake became another pairing. Foote was with Scott Niedermayer, while Jovanovski slotted in for the occasional shift.

Martin Brodeur would start. Joseph was the backup. The third goalie, Ed Belfour, watched from the stands.

The passive German method clearly stymied Canada early on. The Canadians required 6:40 before putting their first shot on goal. Kariya fired off a weak attempt from the slot that was not much of a test for Germany's 27-year-old goalie Marc Seliger, a Washington Capitals 10th-round selection in 1993 who never played a single minute in the NHL.

The Canadians appeared tight and fumbled early chances. Lindros took a roughing penalty on the first shift. Peca failed to get a shot off on a shorthanded breakaway. Fleury had a path for a good scoring chance but was knocked off balance when he bumped into his linemate, Shanahan.

Finally, Canada busted open the stalemate. Just before the game was to hit the 29th minute, Sakic was left alone in front and Gagne found him with a timely pass. The opening goal came on Canada's 16th shot of the game. Germany's Daniel Kunce (yes, it rhymes with dunce) then took a five-minute major for crunching Smyth headfirst into the glass. Kariya would take advantage to make it 2–0, jumping on a Nolan rebound. Foote drifted in a knuckle-ball floater to increase Canada's lead seconds after Kunce's major penalty expired and 44 seconds following Kariya's goal.

But the Germans refused to retreat. They dented Canada's lead in the third period. Andreas Loth put his team on the board 7:36 in with a shot along the ice. Smyth's Edmonton teammate Jochen Hecht then made the affair tense. His shot on the power play bounced off Brodeur's shoulder and caromed off the butt end of the goalie stick to drop into the goal. Canada's lead had been reduced to one.

This development made for a nervous final 6:06. But the Canadians stayed out of the penalty box to hold on. They outshot the Germans 37–20 to survive against a team that housed only two NHLers in Hecht and Marco Sturm. The latter was Nolan's teammate with the San Jose Sharks.

"I know after the German game we were looking around the room and thinking to ourselves, 'Sure, we see all this talent, but sometimes it just doesn't come together in time,'" Canadian defenceman Al MacInnis told the *Vancouver Province* a few days after the Olympics concluded. "Sometimes it just doesn't happen."

The close call caused concern, as evidenced by the quiet ride in the Gretzky-mobile back to Salt Lake City. There were bright spots, however. The line of Sakic, Iginla, and Gagne proved to be a keeper. Foote enjoyed a masterful game, scoring a goal, and he was a rock on the penalty kill. Smyth also was a fine addition to the lineup. His truculent nature and willingness to take punishment around the opposition's net was a welcome element to the Canadian lineup.

When Kunce smashed Smyth, opening up a gash near his right eye, the power play was a much-needed tonic for Canada.

"I remember sitting on the bench in the second period beside Curtis Joseph," said Smyth. The two knew each other well after three seasons together with the Oilers in the mid-1990s. "I think we finally scored to make it 1–0 and he said something like, 'There will be no team that will beat us the rest of the tournament.'

"I'm thinking we just got spanked by Sweden and this was a tight game. But he was right. We didn't lose another game. In that second game we knew we should have been better. But when you play for Canada, you learn that every team gets up to play you."

Smyth learned this lesson many times. There aren't many players who performed in a Canadian sweater as much as Smyth. To go along with the 1,363 combined regular season and playoff games in the NHL, he suited up for Canada another 86 times. He played for his country in the 1995 World Junior Championship (seven games), in seven consecutive world championships from 1999 to 2005 and for an eighth occasion in 2010 (61), the 2002 and 2006 Olympics (12), and the 2004 World Cup of Hockey (six).

His abundant time in a Canadian sweater earned him the nickname Captain Canada as dubbed by veteran hockey reporter Pierre LeBrun after Smyth's seven world championship appearances in a row. To go with the Olympic gold he won in Salt Lake City, Smyth also won a world junior crown, World Cup of Hockey title, and back-to-back world championships in 2003 and 2004. He was inducted in the IIHF Hall of Fame in 2020 for his international exploits.

"My mind-set the first couple of times was this was awesome to play for your country," Smyth said. "I got to meet guys from around the league. My first one was in Lillehammer and my roommate was Adam Graves. I couldn't have asked for a better guy."

Graves won a Stanley Cup with the 1989–90 Oilers and again with the 1993–94 New York Rangers. Smyth grew up in Banff and was a devoted Oilers enthusiast. Canada seemed destined to win it all in Norway in 1999 with five wins in a row. But Canada failed to advance past the semifinal against the Czechs, losing in a shootout on a goal from Jaroslav Spacek, 15 months after the Hasek showstopper in Nagano.

"Spacek did a rowboat celly," remembered Smyth, who would later play with Spacek in Edmonton and lose in Game 7 of the 2006 Stanley Cup Final against the Carolina Hurricanes. "I learned right there and then how much other countries wanted to beat Canada in hockey.

"I thought if I ever got another chance to be a part of this again, I wanted to be a factor. I wanted to be an asset for Canada."

Graves also left Smyth with a sage piece of veteran advice that spring. He told his young Canadian teammate to keep accepting invitations to play for Canada because it was important for Smyth's development.

"He said you should always be training your mind and training physically to be playing meaningful hockey at this time of the year," Smyth said. "It did help me, especially when we made it to the Final in 2006. I'm glad [Hockey Canada] kept asking me."

Smyth was coming off a 31-goal season in 2000–01, but it was his play at the 2001 World Championship in Hanover, Germany, that moved him into contender status for the Olympic team. Sure, Lowe was the Oilers' general manager at the time, but it was Lanny McDonald, part of the Canadian management team that spring, who was swept off his feet by the play of Smyth and Peca, as well as their leadership.

Smyth went to the Canadian Olympic orientation camp in Calgary in early September 2001 and impressed with a strong start to the 2001–02 season with eight goals and 23 points in his first 20 games, including four game-winners. But in Game 21 on November 16, the world came crashing down on Smyth. Less than two minutes into a 7–1 win against the Blackhawks on a Friday evening in Edmonton, he crashed into the end boards with Chicago defenceman Jon Klemm. Smyth fractured his right ankle. The initial diagnosis was he would miss the next 12 weeks. Gretzky was making his final roster decisions in 29 days.

Smyth had surgery that evening at the Misericordia Hospital, where Dr. David Reid inserted a metal plate and implanted seven screws into the ankle. Only time would tell Smyth if this horrific setback would cost him a chance at the Olympics.

"My dreams were shattered," Smyth said. "I give so much credit to [Oilers athletic therapist] Kenny Lowe [Kevin's older brother]. He told me the night the injury happened, 'Smytty, we'll do everything we can to get you back.' He pushed me. Dr. David Reid and Dr. Dave Magee pushed me, and my wife [Stacey] pushed me. I had so many people on my side."

The Olympics were important to Smyth. He had dreams of playing in the Olympics to go along with the usual Stanley Cup aspirations most young hockey players fantasize about. The story about Smyth when he became a stick boy at Canada's summer camp for the 1984 Canada Cup in Banff, Alberta, is well known. Oilers forward Glenn Anderson accidentally ran over Smyth in the parking lot of a golf course. Smyth, who was unhurt, was hunting for autographs at a Canadian team golf tournament. He bent down to tie his shoe and Anderson didn't see him as he pulled out of his parking spot.

A story that is lesser known is that Smyth became captivated by the Olympic spirit four years later. His parents, Dixie and Jim, gave their son the ultimate present for his 12th birthday, a day at the Winter Games in Calgary. The Olympic torch came through his hometown of Banff a few weeks earlier. In Calgary, he had tickets for the 90-metre men's ski jump competition at Canada Olympic Park and watched England's feel-good story Eddie "the Eagle" Edwards compete. The Great Britain celebrity finished 55th out of 55 jumpers. Smyth also closely followed the Canadian hockey team in 1998, rising in the middle of the night to see how Gretzky and his Oilers teammate at the time, Joseph, performed in Nagano.

A little less than four years later, Smyth floored his Edmonton teammates when he showed up to watch a practice 15 days after the injury and subsequent surgery occurred. He had shed his crutches. There was no cast. He walked without a trace of a limp. He was way ahead of schedule because of his hard work in early morning rehab sessions.

His progress was enough for Lowe to report to Gretzky that Smyth would be ready for Salt Lake City. Kevin Lowe called his left wing five minutes before the press conference was to begin in Toronto to let him know he would be named to the roster. Smyth was back on the ice two days after the Canadian roster was unveiled.

He made his return to action at home against the Rangers on January 2, four weeks ahead of schedule. He played more than 18 minutes. He had another 18 games to get ready before departing for Salt Lake City.

"It meant so much to be part of history," Smyth said.

But in order to be part of history, Canada still had to win. As quiet as the Gretzky-mobile was zipping back to Salt Lake City, there was a calmness and quiet confidence amid the players on the team bus.

What do you expect when some of the best leaders in the game were part of the Canadian team, from captain Lemieux to MacInnis to Yzerman to Blake to Nieuwendyk to Sakic to Pronger to Niedermayer to Brodeur and on and on? This group knew you couldn't turn around a difficult situation with panic. This group knew it would perform at its best in a relaxed state. That's sports psychology 101.

"The leadership was off the charts with Mario and this team," Tambellini said. "It was fun, watching the very best in Canada take on the challenges. They knew it came down to them.

"I remember at one time, and I won't name the player, but one of the players was running around too much out there, playing undisciplined. Yzerman quietly went to the guy and said, 'You don't have to do that for us to win. We're that good.'"

Pat Quinn and the coaching staff deserve plenty of credit for staying calm, too. Sure, Quinn was angered with the lackadaisical play against Sweden. He also was sharp with reporters when pestered about the goaltending situation after the Germany game. Who was going to play in the next game against the Czechs? Would Brodeur remain in goal? Would Curtis Joseph receive a second chance? Quinn tossed a third option into the mix—maybe Ed Belfour would get a shot.

"I love the man," Nieuwendyk said. "Pat was just a good person to be around. I think he deserves a ton of credit for the way he handled the rough start, and really the entire tournament."

Nieuwendyk played for several revered coaches in his Hall of Fame career. He won three Stanley Cups with three different teams and three different coaches in Terry Crisp (Calgary), Ken Hitchcock (Dallas), and Pat Burns (New Jersey). Nieuwendyk also played for Bob Johnson, Doug Risebrough, Dave King, Bob Gainey, and Larry Robinson. He also signed with Toronto so he could play for Quinn in

2003–04 and his final two seasons in Florida for Canadian assistant coach Jacques Martin.

"For me, coming to Toronto after six and a half years in Dallas and one and a half more in New Jersey, I really liked playing Pat's style," said Nieuwendyk, the 1999 Conn Smythe winner. "Pat Burns was a little like [Quinn], too. They were part of the old guard. When they spoke, you listened.

"[Quinn] was a players' coach. He let the players handle the locker room. That's the way I liked it."

Nieuwendyk spent time in management after his playing career. When Martin added the general manager's portfolio to his duties with Florida, he brought in Nieuwendyk as a front-office consultant for a season. He then joined the Maple Leafs as a special assistant to GM Cliff Fletcher. Nieuwendyk then gained more experience as the assistant GM for Canada at the 2009 World Championship before becoming the GM in Dallas in June 2009. He lasted four seasons there.

"In management, you're constantly debating why is this coach better than this one," said Nieuwendyk, who worked four more years as a pro scout with the Carolina Hurricanes after his stint as the Dallas GM. "With Pat, some people felt he was too old-school and not technical enough. But that's why you have assistant coaches. Terry Crisp was not a technical coach, but he had Pierre Page and Tom Watt and Doug Risebrough. It just worked. It was the same with Pat Burns in New Jersey with John MacLean and Bobby Carpenter.

"A good coach commands the respect of his players and allows the team to evolve on its own. Pat certainly had those qualities and his presence made him a good coach. You wanted to play hard for him, and you wanted to win for him. I had coaches who were in your face and wouldn't let you breathe. Some players respond to that way. I preferred Pat's style."

The 1998 Canadian Olympic coaching staff of Marc Crawford and his assistants of Andy Murray, Wayne Cashman, and Mike Johnston, as well as video coach Rob Cookson, were connected and knew each other well. Johnston and Cookson were longtime national team coaches. Johnston would later become Crawford's assistant in Vancouver and Los Angeles. Murray and Cashman both had stints as assistant coaches in Philadelphia when Bob Clarke was the GM.

Nicholson and Gretzky decided to make wholesale changes to the coaching staff for 2002. There were no carryovers from 1998. Oddly, there weren't many connections with Quinn, Hitchcock, Martin, Fleming, and Pelino. Of course, Pelino and Fleming knew each other well from their days together with the Canadian national team program. Hitchcock and Fleming had an association, too. Hitchcock would often lend a helping hand to Fleming at summer camps with various Hockey Canada programs.

Fleming made a massive impression during his time with Canada at the 2002 Olympics. Hitchcock would hire him as an assistant coach when the former took over the Philadelphia Flyers in the summer of 2002. Quinn brought in Fleming in his season behind the Edmonton Oilers bench in 2009–10. When Steve Yzerman took over the GM reins of the Tampa Bay Lightning, Fleming was lured to join head coach Guy Boucher's staff.

Hitchcock knew Quinn only from coaching against him in the NHL. Quinn once interviewed Hitchcock when he was coaching junior hockey with the Kamloops Blazers for a position in Vancouver. Quinn also invited Hitchcock to help out at a Canucks training camp.

As far as Hitchcock and Martin were concerned, their history dated back to the 1986 Memorial Cup in Portland, Oregon. But they didn't know each other well. Martin's Guelph Platers, led by Steve Chiasson and Gary Roberts, won the Ontario Hockey League championship. Hitchcock's Blazers, led by Rob Brown and Greg Hawgood, claimed the Western Hockey League crown. The Platers defeated Kamloops in the four-team tournament opener 5–3 and went on to win the championship with a 6–2 victory against a stacked Hull Olympiques team that contained future NHLers Luc Robitaille, Sylvain Cote, Stephane Matteau, and Cam Russell.

In a strange twist, the Olympiques were owned by Gretzky at the time.

The Martin-Quinn combination was also a curious situation because at the time Quinn was at the helm in Toronto and Martin ran the bench of the provincial rival Ottawa Senators. Martin was well liked in the coaching fraternity. But sadly for him, he missed out on a chance to win a Stanley Cup on Crawford's staff with the Colorado Avalanche when he departed from the contender that housed Sakic, Blake, Foote, and Roy midway though the 1995–96 season to coach the Senators. The Avalanche proceeded to win the Stanley Cup that spring. The struggling Senators only won 10 of 38 outings with their new coach to finish last overall.

The Senators slowly improved under Martin. He steered them to eight consecutive playoff appearances, and he won the 1998–99 Jack Adams Award as NHL coach of the year. But Quinn's Maple Leafs would eliminate Martin's Senators in the first round of the playoffs in 2000, sweep them in 2001, and deliver a crushing seven-game victory thanks to a 19-save Curtis Joseph shutout in the 3–0 series finale two months after the Salt Lake City Games.

"It was kind of funny to wind up on the same team together," Martin said. "I knew him a little from before. I considered him a friend, but we weren't close. Even though I coached in Ottawa and he was in Toronto, I always found him to be so friendly. Being together for this tournament was an opportunity to grow our relationship and learn from each other. He was so classy."

Martin and the Senators did upend Hitchcock and the Flyers in 2003 in six games in the second round. Quinn and Martin clashed one final time in the 2004 postseason. Again, it was a long, hard-fought series and required a seventh and deciding game. This time Nieuwendyk starred in the lead role with a pair of first-period goals in Toronto's 4–1 victory.

Martin was fired after the heartbreak finish. He was then hired by the Panthers. One of the first moves Martin cajoled Panthers GM Mike Keenan to make was to sign Nieuwendyk and his old junior talent, Gary Roberts, away from Quinn and the Maple Leafs. Martin also finally earned that elusive Stanley Cup ring—back-to-back rings, in fact—as an assistant coach with the Pittsburgh Penguins in 2015–16 and 2016–17.

Before Salt Lake City, Hitchcock already had a Stanley Cup ring in his possession, steering Nieuwendyk and Belfour to a league title in 1998–99. Anybody who spent time in Edmonton, like Lowe and Gretzky, knew about Ken Hitchcock's success in Sherwood Park (a suburb of Edmonton) with the AAA midget program there. He moved on to Kamloops in 1984 and in six seasons there he won two league championships for two trips to the Memorial Cup.

His first job in the NHL was as an assistant coach in Philadelphia. His third year there was Lindros' rookie season. Gainey hired him away to coach in the minors, and it wasn't long before Hitchcock was the Stars' head coach and winning the Stanley Cup.

The Stanley Cup was something that eluded Quinn in his NHL coaching stops in Philadelphia, Los Angeles, Vancouver, Toronto, and Edmonton. There were close calls. He guided the Maple Leafs to appearances in the East final twice, in 1999 and 2002. Quinn also suffered heartbreak in the Stanley Cup Final, first in 1979–80 in his first season at the helm of the Philadelphia Flyers and again 24 years later with the Vancouver Canucks.

In 1979–80, Quinn had coached the Flyers to a record 35-game unbeaten streak with 25 wins and 10 ties. But Quinn's friendly demeanour would change in a hurry when you brought up the subject of the 1980 Final against the New York Islanders. He could badger on-ice officials with the best of them, but if you wondered about the origin of his disdain for referees and linesmen, look no further than Game 6 between the Flyers and Islanders. The Islanders won that series at Nassau County Coliseum that night—their first of four in a row—on two missed offside calls.

The first non-call was in the first period when a Clark Gillies drop pass off the rush back to Butch Goring appeared to come outside the line. But the play went undetected and was allowed to continue as Duane Sutter put the Islanders ahead 2–1. The second missed call was in overtime on Bob Nystrom's championship-winning goal. It was a difficult play to tell for sure if it was offside, but with all the camera angles for video review in today's game, who knows.

When the Maple Leafs defeated the Islanders 4–1 in Quinn's 800th career NHL game as a head coach, he was still bitter about linesman Leon Stickle's missed call on the Nystrom goal.

"This building still owes me one. I got stiffed here," Quinn said. "Maybe that's why I don't like [officials]."

The 1994 Final between Quinn's Canucks and Kevin Lowe's Rangers produced pure heartbreak for Quinn. After falling behind 3–1 in the series, the Canucks stormed back with decisive 6–3 and 4–1 victories at Madison Square Garden and the Pacific Coliseum, respectively. Mike Richter, a goalie who would become all too familiar to Canadian hockey fans in 1996 and 2002, had the Rangers in front 2–0 at home until Canucks captain Trevor Linden scored a short-handed goal early in the second period.

Linden was foiled by Richter a few shifts later. Rangers captain Mark Messier put his team back up by two goals. Linden would score again, this time with the man advantage on a nifty passing play with Cliff Ronning and Geoff Courtnall. But the goal with 15 minutes and 10 seconds remaining was as close as the Canucks would get. Lowe celebrated his sixth and final Stanley Cup.

The 2002 Canadian Olympic coaching staff had plenty of time to become familiar with each other. The coaching staff was named on the same day Gretzky and Lowe were appointed to the management team in November 2000. The coaching staff assembled to talk shop at the NHL All-Star Game in Denver the first weekend in February 2001. Martin was coach of the World team, led by Dominik Hasek.

Quinn and his staff would meet again in Banff, about six weeks before the orientation camp in Calgary. The group did not need any time to put aside their differences. They combed through the Clarke debriefing document. Fleming and Pelino broke down the opposition. They were a few weeks removed from the 2001 World Championship. Fleming was the head coach and Pelino was an assistant in Hanover, Germany.

"We had Ryan Smyth, Eric Brewer, and Michael Peca from that 2001 team who also played in Salt Lake City," Pelino said. "Peca was probably our best player until he was injured in the final game of the first round."

It was determined in Banff that Quinn, Martin, and Hitchcock would be on the bench in Salt Lake City. Fleming would be in the stands and in radio contact with any sage advice to Hitchcock. Quinn would change the forward lines, Martin the defence pairings.

Hitchcock ran the power play. Martin provided the penalty kill philosophy.

"Pat is the type of guy who empowers the assistants on his staff to do the detail stuff, to do the individual work with players," Hitchcock said. "He had no fear of delegating.

"He really impressed me in our time together. Every coach in that group was a good coach with a lot of good opinions. Sometimes that sort of make-up doesn't work. But Pat acted like we were no threat to him."

Quinn, Hitchcock, and the rest of the coaching staff had their share of input on the roster decisions. They were next going to meet at the 2002 NHL All-Star Game in Los Angeles, two weeks before the Olympic opener against Sweden. Hitchcock, however, was hit with a setback. He was fired as coach of the Stars after seven seasons in Dallas and a Stanley Cup in 1998–99. Hitchcock cajoled the Stars to the final again a year later, but Brodeur and the New Jersey Devils came out on top in 1999–2000. Hitchcock was shown the door after 50 games and a record of 23–17–10 in 2001–02. His fate was sealed after Dallas dropped a 4–2 decision at home against Vancouver on January 23, 2002, 23 days before the puck dropped for Canada in Salt Lake City.

Hitchcock was devastated. He and his family bolted town. They landed in Vail, Colorado. The Stars held a few training camps at the scenic ski destination. Hitchcock had a friend there who put him up in a resort. While his family skied, he perused video on the Olympic front and there were a few job opportunities in the NHL he investigated by watching the games of the interested parties.

He decided the NHL could wait. Instead, he decided to join Quinn and the others in Los Angeles for another strategy session. It was at the All-Star Game that Fleming persuaded Hitchcock to arrive in Salt Lake City 10 days before Canada's opener to scout teams like Belarus, Germany, and Slovakia in the final qualifying round.

Meanwhile, Fleming arrived at the E Center for the first time to find a subpar dressing room. A renovation was required. It was a stroke of good fortune that Don Hay was the head coach of the Utah Grizzlies that season. The Grizzlies were the AHL affiliate of the Dallas Stars and a former assistant of Hitchcock's in Kamloops.

Even though the Olympics dislodged Hay and the Grizzlies on a 17-game, monthlong road trip, Hay made arrangements with local contacts to help Fleming re-paint, re-carpet, and reconfigure the dressing room. At the E Center, each team had a small dressing room to change and shower. But before games they would move into one of the two main dressing rooms for use during the games.

"It was a strange set-up," said Hitchcock, who drove back and forth between Provo and Salt Lake City to take in a selection of the 12 games over four days.

Canada, of course, wound up playing Germany and Belarus in Salt Lake City. Although the Canadians weren't at their best when they played the Germans in the second game, having Fleming and Hitchcock familiar with these two countries helped the cause.

The question, however, after that second game against Germany was whether Lemieux and his teammates could skate their way out of an early tournament funk. Hitchcock felt one of the turning points was when Lemieux and a few of the other veterans pulled the coaching staff aside to tell them practices weren't necessary for the rest of the tournament. If Canada was to advance to the gold medal final, it would have four games and three days off the rest of the way. The off days would be the days before the quarterfinals, semifinals, and final.

"We didn't have a favourable schedule in terms of players arriving in Salt Lake City," Hitchcock said. "We were a tired bunch. We were not up to pace in the Sweden game. We had no energy and were two steps behind. Against Germany, we still were not up to pace. It was apparent we needed rest.

"The veteran leaders who came up to us said, 'You have to trust us.' Going to practice was a pain in the ass because of all the security. It was like a three-hour show for a 30-minute skate. 'You have to trust us on this. We know what to do. You give us the game plan and we'll sell it to the rest of the group.'

"This was a veteran team that knew how to win. They wanted a chance to rest and promised to be better and better. I found there was a tremendous amount of camaraderie between the players and coaches on this team."

In fact, Hitchcock revealed that as the tournament progressed, Quinn and his staff had to do less and less coaching, especially between periods. From the coaches' room they could hear the chatter amongst the players. All the right things were being uttered. Hitchcock singled out Blake as one of the most respected voices in the dressing room.

"He sounded like a coach. He was amazing," Hitchcock recalled. "We said very little between periods. The players were saying the same things we were saying to each other.

"There was no one in the world that was going to beat us, and it started with the next game against the Czechs."

Sharing the experience in Salt Lake City with Quinn were his wife, Sandra, and daughters, Val and Kalli. Kalli was around her dad quite a bit in the Olympic bid. She had been hired by Hockey Canada to take care of the 189-person contingent of family members who were in Salt Lake City to cheer on their son, brother, cousin, or husband. She arranged tickets to other events, sightseeing tours, and dinners. The Canadian team brass wanted to keep distractions to a minimum for the players. If their families were taken care of, the players could focus on the games.

"We were a lot better prepared on and off the ice in 2002," Theo Fleury said. "What I mean by that, in Nagano, I was worried about my family, what were they doing, were they having a good time, that sort of thing.

"Wayne [Gretzky] took away all the distractions and as a result all we had to do was worry about playing hockey. This is a guy who was so aware about what it takes. Nobody else has his level of awareness."

Kalli Quinn had Olympic dreams as a teenager as a swimmer. She was a member of the Vancouver Dolphins Swim Club and diligently trained at her specialty, the 200-metre backstroke. She was devastated when she failed to qualify for the 1988 Olympic Games at the Canadian trials by less than a second. But her timing proved right 12 years later. She was the executive assistant for general manager David Poile of the Nashville Predators. Nicholson approached Kalli about the position during the Olympics and Poile gave her permission to defect to the Canadian team.

"It was quite the experience," said Kalli, who even had a chance to take in one of her favourite country bands, Brooks and Dunn, at the downtown Medals Plaza venue on the evening before the game against Germany. "I hoped to experience the Olympics as an athlete, a swimmer. But to be alongside my dad for this was something I will never forget. I have so many memories from Salt Lake City."

A memory Gretzky loves to share about his cigar-smoking head coach occurred in the aftermath following the fury of the Sweden game. His anger was evident in his postgame session with reporters. But he flushed his disappointment, turning to humour.

In the days leading up to his departure for Salt Lake City, Quinn had seen a Molson Canadian commercial on television. The 30-second spot showed a bunch of Canadians on a bus crossing the border. A customs officer asked if there was anything to declare. "Just this big old can of whoop ass," the Canadian answered.

Quinn loved it. So when he ran into Gretzky, still wearing the weight of the world on his shoulders from the Sweden loss, he told the Great One not to worry, that he had a big old can of whoop ass. He then taped up an aerosol can before the Germany game and wrote "Whoop Ass" on it. He showed the players his prop and the bit did the trick, producing a few chuckles around the dressing room.

Quinn shared his Olympic mind-set a few years following Salt Lake City in Mike Johnston and Ryan Walter's 2004 book, *Simply the Best: Insights and Strategies from Great Hockey*. The authors interviewed many great coaches, including Clare Drake, Scotty Bowman, Roger Neilson, and Quinn.

"I was bothered the whole summer about how I would approach this because I knew [the fear] was going to be there," said Quinn, who added he felt terrible for the criticism directed at Bobby Clarke and Marc Crawford after the shootout flop in Nagano.

"That fear is a powerful thing. All the good teams had to learn it—Detroit, the Islanders, the great Oiler teams—they all had to learn how to perform and win when the pressure was on. It's a learning process. Nobody can just walk in and say, 'Here's how you do it, guys.' You've got to lose, you've got to battle, you've got to feel the pain, and then you've got to rise up and come back again."

Many of the Canadian players recalled how every night on the way back to the Olympic Village, Quinn would be sitting outside on a bench puffing on his trademark cigar. Sometimes another Canadian athlete would sit beside the burly hockey coach on the piece of furniture that later had a sign stuck on it by a volunteer: PAT'S BENCH.

Quinn was curious about the new friends/athletes who would sit down for a chat. Sometimes the sessions would conclude with the Canadian skier or skater or bobsleigh athlete asking for advice. Quinn's counsel always was the same: don't worry about what others think; your gut instinct will push you in the right direction.

Fittingly, when the Canucks honoured Quinn with a statue in February 2017, sculptor Norm Williams added Pat's bench to commemorate his time in Salt Lake City.

Sadly, the hockey world lost Fleming and Quinn in 2013 and 2014, respectively. Fleming was diagnosed with brain cancer shortly before the 2011 Stanley Cup playoffs. When Hitchcock was named the 2011–12 Jack Adams Award winner a few months later, he dedicated his Coach of the Year honour to his former assistant. Fleming passed away in his Calgary home on March 25, 2013, at age 62.

Quinn succumbed after a lengthy illness 18 months later at age 71. He had been named chairman of the Hockey Hall of Fame board on August 1, 2013. But due to his ill health, Quinn was unable to attend the 2014 induction ceremonies, in which the international class of Blake, Hasek, Peter Forsberg, and Mike Modano—all Olympians— were inducted. Quinn passed away a couple weeks later, on November 23, 2014. He was inducted into the Hockey Hall of Fame two years later with Rogie Vachon, Eric Lindros, and Russian great Sergei Makarov. Vachon was a rookie GM when he hired Quinn to coach the Kings in 1984. Lindros, of course, played for Quinn on the 2002 Canadian Olympic team.

"He didn't talk a lot about what happened in the room," Kalli said. "He did say he was getting a lot of pressure from everywhere. But he wasn't going to let it get to him. He had this belief in the players. He believed he had the right guys and if they would just stick to the game plan, we'd be all right.

"I still get teary-eyed thinking about all the memories. I remember sitting with him on a bench outside the Hale Center [where the Canadian players gathered with family and friends after games] after the Belarus game saying, 'Dad, you're going to be an Olympic medalist.' He said back, 'There's only one colour I want, and it's not silver.'"

CHAPTER 5

CUJO CZECHS OUT

Ten months before the 2002 Winter Games, Curtis Joseph and Martin Brodeur stood at opposite ends of the rink, ready to clash in the second round of the 2001 Stanley Cup playoffs.

When executive director Wayne Gretzky and his management team named their eight early selections for the Canadian Olympic team, there wasn't a goalie among the choices on March 23, 2001. Instead, the initial spots on the roster went to veteran forwards Paul Kariya, Mario Lemieux, Owen Nolan, Joe Sakic, Steve Yzerman, and defencemen Rob Blake, Scott Niedermayer, and Chris Pronger.

The goaltending competition for No. 1 was wide open with Joseph, Brodeur, Ed Belfour, and Patrick Roy as the main contenders. Belfour (1999), Brodeur (2000), and Roy (2001) were the last three Canadian goalies to have won the Stanley Cup.

Joseph had a knack for pushing mediocre teams in St. Louis, Edmonton, and Toronto to better-than-expected results in the playoffs, like he did with the Maple Leafs in 1999 when they advanced to the East final. When his career concluded, his 454 regular season victories ranked fifth on the all-time list, and his 63 playoff wins were tops among netminders without a Stanley Cup ring.

Roy was the Olympic incumbent. He played every minute of the 1998 Winter Games. Joseph and Brodeur backed up St. Patrick with Brodeur on the bench and Joseph in the stands.

But Roy would bow out early from the 2002 race. He informed Gretzky on November 21, 2001, with a morning phone call that he no longer had the Olympic spirit. Roy wanted to employ the three-week break to rest up for the playoffs and a run at a fifth Stanley Cup championship. He was bothered by a hip injury early in the 2001–02 campaign and only won four of his first 13 starts. But after a concerning 0–6–1 slump he was the victor in three of his next five outings, including three shutouts in a row, before his call to Gretzky.

The game that ended his shutout streak was a 5–3 loss to the New York Rangers at Madison Square Garden, in which Roy was lifted after surrendering the fifth goal on 18 shots midway through the second period.

Before the game, *New York Post* columnist Larry Brooks asked Rangers forward Theo Fleury who he felt was the leading candidate to be Canada's No. 1 goalie at the Olympics.

"We'll see how it stands after the game," Fleury replied. "We might know more then."

Theories abound as to why Roy pulled the chute. But the smart money said that Roy wanted to be guaranteed the No. 1 spot, something Gretzky and head coach Pat Quinn refused to promise.

"It would not matter to me to be No. 1 or No. 2," Roy said.

He had a history. At the 1987 Canada Cup, after Mike Keenan informed the four goalies in training camp that Grant Fuhr had been anointed as Canada's No. 1 netminder, Roy bolted training camp in a huff, leaving Ron Hextall and Kelly Hrudey as the backups.

Roy informed his Avalanche teammates the day after his Madison Square Garden outing that he no longer wanted to compete for a spot on the Canadian roster. Rob Blake, Adam Foote, and Joe Sakic had particular interest because Blake and Sakic already had been named to the club for Salt Lake City. Foote was a strong contender. He also played for Canada four years earlier in Nagano.

Foote was Roy's longtime roommate on the road. But neither he nor Blake nor Sakic attempted to talk their All-Star goalkeeper out of his decision.

"We had just gone to the Final and he wanted to make sure he was ready for the playoffs again," Sakic said. "He also wanted some time off to watch his son play in the Quebec Pee-Wee tournament."

The Quebec Pee-Wee tournament in Quebec City is the biggest stage in the world for hockey players aged 11–12. Guy Lafleur played in the tournament. Roy, Steve Yzerman, and Mario Lemieux competed against one another in the 1977 edition.

Roy's 12-year-old son, Jonathan, also a goalie, played for a team from Colorado. Patrick wound up opening and closing the door on his son's bench during the tournament.

"We would have liked to have him, but how do you question him after hearing those two reasons?" Sakic reasoned.

Roy waited until after the Avalanche's outing that evening on Long Island on November 21, a 5–4 loss to the Islanders in which Roy backed up David Aebischer. There had been whispers circulating around the Avalanche for a week or so that Roy would drop out of the Olympics.

"It's no longer a rumour," Roy told reporters. "My reasons are simple. I wanted to take the time to prepare myself to have a good playoff and finish the season strongly."

Roy remarked the Stanley Cup always has been his No. 1 motivation.

"An Olympic gold medal has never been part of my dreams the way the Stanley Cup has been my whole life," he said.

"I was there [in the Olympics] before and certainly want to give the chance to another guy to play. When you look at the quality of goaltending that there is, I have no doubt that they will be fine and they will have great goaltending."

Roy was 36. He also told Gretzky that this might be his last season. He would play one more season, but to his disappointment there would be no fifth Stanley Cup championship to celebrate.

How did he fare in 2002 after his Olympic break? Roy helped the Avalanche advance all the way to the West final against the rival Detroit Red Wings. He had Colorado ahead three games to two after a 26-save 2–1 overtime win in Detroit.

The final two games were a different story. The Red Wings blanked the Avalanche 2–0 and 7–0 to take the series and move on to the Stanley Cup Final. Guess who beat Roy with back-to-back shutouts in the final two games? The same guy who had cost Roy and Canada a shot at Olympic gold in 1998—Dominik Hasek.

Gretzky, at least publicly, took Roy's news as well as could be expected.

"He was open and honest and direct with me," Gretzky told the *Toronto Sun* on the day Roy placed his withdrawal call. "He said he wanted to rest.

"I respect his decision. Obviously, he was one of the goalies that we were looking at, but the other three goalies we had in camp are very capable as well."

But Gretzky's difficult time with the goaltending situation didn't end with Roy's bombshell. Five days later, a *New York Post* story reported that Brodeur also was disgruntled with the Canadian Olympic team. The report suggested Brodeur was not considered a top pick by Canada for the Olympics because Brodeur's superior puck-handling ability, one of his many skills, would not be useful against European teams on the larger ice surface.

"He's the best puck-handling goaltender, but that didn't come into play much in the last Olympics," the *New York Post* quoted an unnamed Canadian official. "For one thing, teams don't dump the puck much on an Olympic rink. And the corners are more square in the Olympics, so pucks that are dumped in the corners stay in the corners."

Gretzky phoned Brodeur that day to ensure the two-time Stanley Cup winner—at the time—that he was very much in the mix.

"First of all, that's absolutely ridiculous," Gretzky told Canadian television network *Sportsnet* two days after the initial report. "That's a ludicrous report. There was no substance behind it, no validation behind it. It's the craziest thing I've ever heard or read.

"We immediately contacted Martin. I mean the guy's won two Stanley Cups, lost in a Game 7 last year in the Stanley Cup Final. He is one of the nicest people you'll ever meet in professional sports.

"I felt really bad for him that somebody would say something so unfounded."

For his part, Brodeur later made it official that he would suit for Canada in Salt Lake City whether he was the starter or the backup.

"I've decided to accept an invitation if it's offered, no matter what," Brodeur told the *New York Post*. "If not No. 1, maybe No. 2, maybe No. 3.

"I'm pretty sure I'll be there. No. 3, it's up in the air, but I'll accept it."

Back to late April 2001: Brodeur versus Joseph provided an intriguing Canadian Olympic team backdrop for the seven-game series between the Toronto Maple Leafs and New Jersey Devils.

Brodeur prevailed. But Joseph was excellent early on in the series as Toronto built a 3–2 lead. The Maple Leafs hopes of advancement to the conference final were finished late in Game 4 when Toronto enforcer Tie Domi targeted Scott Niedermayer with a vicious elbow.

The Devils were hot, furious. They lost Niedermayer for the next game with a concussion. Domi was suspended for the rest of the play-offs and the first eight games of the next regular season.

The Maple Leafs won Game 5 with Niedermayer on the sidelines. But with the smooth-skating defenceman back in action the Devils responded with victories in the next two outings by a combined score of 9–3. Brodeur and the Devils would advance to the Stanley Cup Final, but they lost to Roy and the Avalanche in seven games.

Little separated the performances of Joseph and Brodeur in the first four months of the 2001–02 season. In fact, neither were in fine form. That also was the case with Ed Belfour.

If anyone distinguished himself and was deserving of a roster spot it was Sean Burke. The Phoenix Coyotes netminder was six weeks shy of his 35th birthday when Canada's Olympic team roster was unveiled. But he clearly was among the game's best through the first three months of the season with an 11–6–7 record and .924 save percentage with a middling Coyotes club.

In comparison, Joseph had steered Toronto to third overall in the league standings through mid-December with a 17–9–2 record and .911 save percentage. Brodeur hit mid-December in better form but still only sported a 13–12–3 record and .895 save percentage. Belfour had a 9–9–6 record and .897 save percentage for Dallas.

Brodeur wasn't concerned with his mediocre start. He believed the No. 1 spot would go to the goalie playing the best leading up to the Olympic Games.

"Whoever is hot right now, that doesn't mean they're going to be hot in February," Brodeur said during an NHL-organized conference call a few days before Christmas. "The test will start in February, and it's going to last for two weeks."

There wasn't much to distinguish the members of the trio with their play in those two weeks before arriving in Salt Lake City. Belfour went 2–2–1 in early February with a .915 save percentage. Brodeur had gone 2–1–2 with a .918 save percentage. Joseph played in only three outings, going 2–1–0 with a .930 save percentage.

Quinn decided to go with his guy, Joseph, as No. 1. Brodeur would back up. Belfour was given the role of the third goalie over Burke. Canadian assistant coach Ken Hitchcock stuck up for his Dallas netminder.

"Let's get to the heart of it," Hitchcock said during the roster-selection debate in mid-December as recorded for a CBC documentary. "I've had Belfour for five years and I believe in the guy. He hasn't been great this year, but neither has Brodeur. If something happened to, say, Cujo, if he was No. 1, Eddie could win a game for us. He has the ability to shut out the whole world to win a game."

Two decades later, Hitchcock outlined Quinn's decision to go with Joseph as the starter.

"The decision on the starting goalie was up to Pat," Hitchcock said. "We felt we had three very strong goalies."

Hitchcock was asked to make sure Belfour understood he would be in the stands for the games unless there was an injury.

"Eddie had never been in that position before, but he was great in accepting it," said Hitchcock, who won a Stanley Cup with Belfour and the Dallas Stars three years earlier.

The only other time the native of Carmen, Manitoba represented his country was at the 1991 Canada Cup as part of a triumvirate that included Bill Ranford and Burke. But Ranford played every minute of Canada's seven games and was named the tournament MVP.

"I would have loved to have played in Salt Lake City," Belfour said. "But it wasn't in the cards. For me, it was an honour to be named to the team and be part of a group of determined guys who came together when it mattered the most to win."

Joseph and Brodeur knew each other and admired each other's talent. They were teammates at the 1996 World Championship in Vienna when Canada settled for a silver medal and again several months later in Canada's loss to the United States in the best-of-three World Cup of Hockey final. Joseph was the No. 1 goalie for Canada and enjoyed a strong 1996 World Cup tournament. They again were teammates at the 1998 Olympics.

"I admire Marty," Joseph said. "He's smart, very sharp. I always enjoyed talking with him. But these events are such short-term periods of time when you're friends and teammates. There is no sharing of secrets. There is camaraderie, sharing of stories, the ride, some laughs, and seriousness."

The two elite-level goalies were pals, but not bosom buddies. Joseph was five years older and the two had travelled much different paths before being named teammates for a fourth time. Brodeur was a prodigy. His career in hockey was predetermined.

His Dad, Denis, was the official photographer of the Montreal Canadiens. As a youth, Martin was omnipresent at Habs practices and games at the old Montreal Forum. He knew from an early age he wanted to become the next Patrick Roy.

Brodeur was the Devils' first-round selection (20th overall) in 1990 and before his 20th birthday he already had notched his first NHL regular season victory and saw some playoff action in relief a month later.

Brodeur won the Calder Trophy and a pair of Stanley Cups by the time the Salt Lake City Games rolled around. Joseph was another story. The man known as Cujo had to scratch and claw for his pro career.

He was born five years and seven days before Brodeur in Keswick, Ontario, just north of Toronto. Curtis was adopted by nurse Jeanne Joseph, five days after he was born to teenage parents Wendy Munro and Curtis Nickle.

Joseph was never drafted. He was the only undrafted player on the Canadian roster. He signed his first NHL contract with the St. Louis Blues at age 22 after his freshman season at the University of Wisconsin. He began his rookie pro campaign with the Peoria Rivermen of the International Hockey League and was promoted in early January when the Blues ran into goaltender problems.

Joseph won six of his first eight regular season outings and upended the Maple Leafs in the first round of the 1990 playoffs. He usually was at his best in the playoffs, even though the furthest he had advanced was the 1999 Eastern Conference final with the Maple Leafs.

Like most Canadian hockey players, the thought of winning an Olympic gold medal did not enter Joseph's mind until the NHL decided to participate in the Winter Games for the first time in 1998. But Brodeur had a different mind-set. He always yearned to play in the Olympics.

Every time he walked through the family living room in his Montreal home, he passed by the bronze medal his dad claimed while with the Kitchener-Waterloo Dutchmen, the amateur senior team that represented Canada at the 1956 Olympics in Cortina d'Ampezzo, Italy.

"Every time the Olympics came around it was a special time for my dad and the family," Brodeur said. "He never played pro hockey. This was his big accomplishment. I grew up with my dad's medal hanging up in the living room.

"When I started my NHL career, the opportunity to play in the Olympics wasn't there for NHL players. This was a dream come true."

Denis shared his son's experience in Nagano, and he was there four years later in Salt Lake City. The Devils goalie honoured his dad on his mask in 2002 with a reference to the bronze medal won 46 years earlier.

Even though the younger Brodeur did not play in Canada's 3–2 loss to Finland in the bronze medal game in Nagano, he regretted Canada mailing in its effort in the third-place game.

"[Dad] always said to me any colour of medal was something that would stay with you the rest of your life," said Brodeur, who, as assistant GM of the 2018 Canadian Olympic team, relayed this message to the players as they prepared for their bronze medal game against the Czech Republic. The words of wisdom were heard loud and clear as the Canadians defeated the Czechs 6–4 to finish third.

"You never know if it's your last opportunity of your career," Brodeur said. "For me, that was special."

His bronze medal is on display in his home with the Olympic gold medals he won in 2002 and eight years later in Vancouver.

But there was a time when Brodeur wondered if he would ever receive a shot to perform in the Olympics. In 1998, Colorado Avalanche bench boss Marc Crawford was the Canadian head coach. He chose to start his goalie, Roy, over Brodeur. With Quinn in charge, Brodeur had an inkling Joseph was No. 1.

"The first two times I went to the Olympics I had Patrick Roy and Crawford, and Quinn and Joseph," Brodeur said. "I was thinking, 'That's not good.'

"I understood the situation for Pat. But I wanted to play, too."

Brodeur chatted with Gretzky prior to the tournament. The goalie wanted assurance that he would start at least one game. The Great One gave him his word that would be the case. Brodeur would see action.

It was up to Quinn and his coaching staff to come up with a blueprint. So after a few conference calls prior to arriving in Salt Lake City, the plan was for Joseph to start the tournament opener against Sweden and Brodeur would play against Germany two nights later with Joseph back in goal for the final game of the preliminary round against the Czech Republic.

Sometimes, however, plans need to be revised. And after Joseph surrendered five consecutive goals by Sweden, both Joseph and Brodeur had a feeling that the tournament now was the latter's moment of truth.

"Marty was a Hall of Famer, or at least we all knew he was going to the Hall of Fame," Joseph said. "I figured he was going to get a shot to continue. You only get one shot in these high-level tournaments. The problem with being a goaltender is only one can play."

Joseph admits he wasn't at his best against Sweden. But he didn't deserve all the blame. The rest of the group played loose in front of him in the 5–2 defeat.

"It would be hard to point a finger and say we've got to change the goaltending," Quinn said afterward, "because we didn't play very well in front of him.

"He didn't let five in. He had a lousy defensive team in front of him."

"I don't think I let any bad ones in," Joseph added. "But you're a professional, and any time you let five go by you, you're not happy."

Although he disagrees, Joseph could be faulted on only one of the five goals, the second from his Maple Leafs teammate Mats Sundin at the midpoint of the second period. Sweden enjoyed a three-on-two break for the 3–1 goal. Sundin beat Joseph with a slapper from the top of the faceoff circle to the right of the Canada goal.

Sundin's first goal came on a stretch pass between the Canadian defence duo of Al MacInnis and Eric Brewer for a breakaway. Niklas Sundstrom was left unchecked in front by Canada's Joe Sakic for the 2–1 goal.

After Sundin put the Tre Kronor in front 3–1, Sweden had another odd-man rush. This time, a two-on-one. Henrik Zetterberg hit a trailing Kenny Jonsson for a three-goal lead. The Swedes increased their lead to four goals after Ulf Dahlen skated in behind Pronger off a rush that was generated by a stretch pass from Sundin to Sundstrom.

"I felt bad for Cujo," Canadian defenceman Adam Foote said. "We weren't ready. The coaching staff had us ready. But we were tired from getting to Salt Lake City the day before and an exhausting first day there."

"We hung Cujo out to dry," Sakic added. "We got away from our game. But we were confident in either Cujo or Marty."

Brodeur, meanwhile, bumped into Gretzky after the disappointment of the Sweden game.

"He told me, 'Now it's your tournament to lose,'" Brodeur recalled.

Brodeur did win his first Olympic start. But the 3–2 victory was unremarkable. The Canadians hung on for a nervous victory. They almost squandered a three-goal lead when Germany scored twice in the final period; Jochen Hecht made it 3–2 with a fluky marker with 6:10 remaining in the third. The German's shot deflected off a

Canadian defender, then bounded off Brodeur's shoulder and off the butt of his stick into the goal.

So it wasn't a slam dunk that Brodeur would be back in goal for the third game, even if Gretzky remarked after the Germany game not to anticipate any change after Brodeur won. There still were issues to be resolved in the next 48 hours before Canada's final preliminary round against the Czechs.

Did Joseph deserve a second chance? After all, the original plan was for Joseph to play against Sweden, give way to Brodeur for the second game, and then for Joseph to return to the No. 1 role in the third game against the Czechs. But given the results so far, should Canada stick with Brodeur?

A third option was to put in Belfour. This became a possibility immediately after the Germany game. Quinn was pressed about his net-minding situation by reporters. He was asked who would start against the Czechs.

"Maybe Curtis or we might go with Eddie," Quinn retorted, muddying the state of affairs.

Brodeur was confident he would remain the man after he beat Germany. But Hitchcock admitted no final decision had been made.

"Pat was coaching Curtis in Toronto," Hitchcock said. "But there was a strong case for Marty to stay in. He was having a heck of a year.

"There was worry, worry about what would happen with the relationship between Pat and Curtis if he didn't go back in. We also were worried, what message does this send to the team if Curtis didn't go back in?"

Quinn stood up as the coach's meeting wound down after the Germany game and stated, "I'll deal with Curtis later on. That's between a coach and a player. We have to do what's best for our country and our team."

Hitchcock said, "So we left it up to Pat to make the decision."

Quinn made his decision the next day. Brodeur would continue on. So Quinn had a heart-to-heart with Joseph to explain his decision. There was disappointment for the Maple Leafs goalie, but he understood his coach's difficult dilemma.

The rest of the players, Brodeur included, were informed at a team meeting the night before the Czech game.

"I have the utmost respect and confidence in Curtis," Quinn said in his gold medal press conference a few days later. "We played him in the opening game, we made the change we planned to make for the second game. Once we got through those games, we stuck with Marty. It was part superstition as we were getting better. We weren't going to switch then."

The switch perked up the players. They knew the move from Joseph to Brodeur was a difficult decision for their coach.

"We had a lot of figuring out to do in those first two or three games," Pronger said. "We had to figure out who played best with each other. The coaches had to figure out line combinations, defence pairings, and the starting goalie.

"I don't think Cujo was great against Sweden," Pronger continued. "But I don't think he was terrible. As a team we were not good, we were not in sync. Our chemistry was off. We were all on our own page. I think Cujo getting sacked and Brodeur going in was a wake-up call. We all knew we had to play better because we just cost this guy his job and it became a matter of answering the bell. We had to get going."

The players did get going eventually. It took a while, but Brodeur did not let his teammates down the rest of the way.

"In looking back, I think Marty was the better goalie for us, because of the way he handled the puck," said Foote, debunking that

New York Post story in late November. "He beat the forecheckers to the puck and helped out the D."

"It was a tough deal for [Joseph]," Belfour added. "There was a lot of pride on the line, but the decision proved to be for the best. You want success for everyone. It was unfortunate. It just wasn't our day, and it wasn't Curtis'. That's sports. When things don't go your way, you want to react in a positive manner, and we did."

When the switch was made for good for the rest of the tournament, the players knew Quinn made quite a sacrifice in going with Brodeur over his own. Some, like Pronger, were aware Joseph was eligible for free agency that summer.

"It probably cost Pat Cujo," Pronger concluded. "But at the end of the day, Marty was capable and ready. He had won a couple of Stanley Cups."

Just how icy did the relationship between Quinn and Joseph become after, as Pronger put it, the sacking? On the surface, it seemed irreparable.

First, Joseph went from starter to sitting in the stands for the Czech game. Belfour backed up Brodeur. But the reason for Belfour dressing for Game 3 was to bring him closer to the action in order to make him feel part of the team. Joseph was the backup for each of the three games in the playoff round.

The second such incident occurred back home in Toronto, two nights after the gold medal game, in a pregame ceremony to honour Joseph, Quinn, and gold medal speed skater Catriona Le May Doan. Joseph shook Le May Doan's hand during the ceremony, but then he put his blocker back on his right hand and gave Quinn an awkward fist-bump moments later.

If there wasn't a rift, why didn't Joseph give his coach a heartfelt handshake?

"Yes, there was a lot made of that," Joseph said. "I respect Pat so much. Giving him the blocker as a fist bump sort of thing didn't play out in the media the way it felt to me on the ice."

The Maple Leafs won that night 4–1 against the visiting Carolina Hurricanes. Joseph made 26 saves but exited the game midway through the third period when he stumbled and got his hand caught in the mesh as he tried to regain his balance.

He missed the next six weeks with a broken left hand. Joseph reappeared in time for Toronto's penultimate regular season game. It didn't take him long to regain his form to backstop the Maple Leafs all the way to the conference final.

But the whispers that Joseph was at odds with Quinn would not fade. There was a report that Joseph demanded a trade before the March 19 deadline. That rumour was swiftly shot down by Quinn and Joseph's agent, Don Meehan.

There also were the bumpy negotiations on Joseph's contract extension after the lengthy Maple Leafs playoff run. Joseph's camp wanted four years. Quinn wouldn't budge from the team's three-year, $22 million tender.

Joseph decided to bolt. He signed a three-year, $24 million contract to play with his Olympic teammates Steve Yzerman and Brendan Shanahan and the Detroit Red Wings, the defending Stanley Cup champions. Detroit needed a new No. 1 after Hasek retired.

Joseph's time in Detroit was a disaster. The Red Wings were swept in the first round by the Anaheim Ducks. Hasek then un-retired but failed to get on track in 2003–04 due to a groin injury. Joseph, at one point, was demoted to Grand Rapids of the American Hockey League.

But because of Hasek's ailment Joseph returned to the Red Wings. Manny Legace began the playoffs as Detroit's No. 1, but after he faltered, Joseph was restored to action. He was stellar with a .939

save percentage. The Red Wings, however, were ousted in the second round by the eventual conference-champion Calgary Flames.

Joseph's third year in Detroit was wiped out because of the season-cancelling 2004–05 lockout. He regretted his move to Detroit, but not his Olympic experience.

"No, how can you be bitter?" he said. "The competitive nature in me is like, 'Dang, you get one chance.' But the ultimate goal was to win gold. It's not that easy. There is a ton of pressure, and I can't undermine what a fantastic feat it was to win.

"Any time it's a world stage like that and you're picked to be a part of a team it's an honour. Then you win. Anybody would give their right arm to be a part of that.

"Ultimately, we accomplished something the entire country wanted. Decisions were made, that's fine. It still was a ton of fun."

Would Joseph have done anything different? You bet.

"In hindsight, maybe I needed to stay busier [leading up to the Olympics]," he said. Joseph turned down an invite to the NHL All-Star Game in Los Angeles on February 2.

The week before he flew to Salt Lake City, Joseph played in three games: on February 5 at home against Minnesota; on the road against the New York Islanders on February 7; and in a 4–1 win against Montreal at home on February 9, in which he made 22 saves. Joseph then sat out the Maple Leafs' final game against Atlanta at home prior to the Olympic break. That meant a five-day break for him until the Sweden game.

"I felt I had a little too much time off," Joseph said. "I like to play every game. I didn't go to the All-Star Game and play that last game in Toronto because I didn't want to get hurt.

"Sweden came out quickly. I didn't have my best game. I was a little rusty."

Yes, the relationship between Quinn and Joseph hit a pothole in the offseason during contract negotiations, but the coach praised his goalie's professionalism in the coach's gold medal interview session.

"He's a great kid and I wanted him to do well," said Quinn. "He's happy today. He might have been happier if he was playing. But he was a big part of this gold medal. We had three goalies and we trusted all three of them."

The world of pro hockey is small. Who did Quinn turn to as his new goalie in Toronto after Joseph departed? Belfour.

"I loved the man," Belfour said, referring to his late Maple Leafs head coach. "I didn't know him until the Olympics. He surprised me because here is this big man who actually was relaxed. He treated everybody equally and with respect. He was a true leader.

"He was a big teddy bear. I got to know him at the Olympics and found out what a gentleman he was."

Brodeur found out eight years later in Vancouver what it was like to be Joseph in Salt Lake City. Brodeur lost his status as Canada's No. 1 to Roberto Luongo after a 5–3 loss to the United States in the final game of the preliminary round. Canada eventually won gold in Vancouver. The road is rarely smooth for these gold medal teams. But Joseph and Brodeur will tell you the Olympic gold medal—and representing Canada—is all that matters.

CHAPTER 6

THE RANT

If nerves were frayed among the Canadian contingent in Salt Lake City after the Germany game, they were pushed to the brink of a breakdown in the late stages of the game against the Czech Republic. The Canadians had put forth their best effort in three games. But Jiri Dopita, a 33-year-old teammate of Eric Lindros with the Philadelphia Flyers, put the Czechs in front with a rebound with less than seven minutes remaining in the third period.

Another three minutes elapsed. Was this talent-rich Canadian team ever going to skate its way out of this funk? Win, lose, or draw, the outcome in this game didn't matter. The Canadians would advance no matter what. But for their peace of mind, a positive result would be a much-needed boost to the psyche.

There was one more game to be played on the final day of the preliminary round, the Sweden-Germany matchup. So Canada knew its fate for the quarterfinals before taking on the Czechs. A Canadian win would have meant a quarterfinal date with Russia because Finland scored a 3–1 upset against the Russians early that afternoon. A loss or draw meant Canada would face Finland in two days.

Canada continued to press the Czechs late in the game. Finally, some magic happened. Young defenceman Ed Jovanovski jumped into the play to poke the puck behind the goal. Theo Fleury chased down the prized possession and took a quick peek over his left shoulder to see a linemate moving into some open space. Fleury then swung a pass to Joe Nieuwendyk out front, and all of a sudden the game was tied for the third time. The game finished that way, even at 3–3.

Other than the fact Canada couldn't pull out a win, there were so many boxes to check on the positive side about the Canadian effort. The Czech Republic, after all, was a country on a hockey roll. After their Olympic gold medal victory in Nagano, they followed up with a bronze at the 1998 World Championship and three golden finishes in a row at the Worlds in 1999, 2000, and 2001.

The Czechs were so confident in their counter-attack system. They played a patient game, waiting to pounce on mistakes from the opposition, mistakes they transformed lickety-split into odd-man rushes. It didn't seem to matter who they plugged into the lineup. All the Czechs had familiarity and faith in the system. The amount of victories proved it worked like a charm.

Captain Mario Lemieux scored twice against the Czechs in this critical outing after sitting out the game against Germany. Canada performed at a much better pace. They only took a couple of minor penalties and outshot the Czechs 36–23.

Jovanovski's crafty play to set up the tying goal was another example of how important the young lions were to the success of this veteran Canadian lineup. Canada had the third-oldest roster of the final eight countries that competed in Salt Lake City. The United States were the oldest with an average age of 31 years, 10 months, followed by Belarus at 30 years, five months, and Canada at 30 years, three months.

The oldest Canadian player was Al MacInnis at 38, while the youngest included Ryan Smyth and Jovanovksi, both 25; a 24-year-old Jarome Iginla; Eric Brewer, 22; and Simon Gagne, 21. From the time they were selected and arrived at the orientation camp in Calgary, six months before the Olympics, players like Brewer had to overcome the shock and awe of playing alongside some of his childhood heroes.

"You feel like a fish out of water," admitted Brewer, who was midway through his fourth season in the NHL when he arrived in Salt Lake City. He was raised in Ashcroft, a small village along the scenic Thompson River in the interior of British Columbia.

"For me, this a was big deal. I grew up in the 1980s in a small town. The Oilers and Flames were such high-level teams. I collected hockey cards and had those sticker books. I watched *Hockey Night in Canada* every Saturday. I had watched a majority of these guys play in the late 1980s and early 1990s. To all of sudden be in the same dressing room and to be teammates with them was surreal."

Ask any of the young players on this Canadian team and they have vivid memories of watching how players like Lemieux, Joe Sakic, and Steve Yzerman acted at the rink before and after games as well as team functions.

Before a game, there would be Sakic in a jovial mood, working on his sticks. Yzerman likely would be working on a crossword puzzle. Lemieux would work his way around the dressing room, making sure he would utter a word or two of encouragement to each and every player.

"They made it super easy to be around," Brewer said. "They were all very humble. They had been in my shoes before, so they made sure I was comfortable.

"Don't forget this was a pressure-filled Olympics. It was the first one in North America since 9/11. It was still fresh in everybody's mind. The security was off the charts. You could not go anywhere fast. It had brought everyone a real dose of reality. Yet our leaders were so quiet, so calm. They made you feel so comfortable in the dressing room, at the team dinners, or on the team bus. It didn't matter where you sat."

After every game the Canadian players would meet their families at the nearby Canadian Hockey House and sit down for some postgame grub. Brewer recalled how after one of the games, Yzerman sat down beside him to talk shop.

"I don't exactly remember the details about what we talked about, but he was curious to get my thoughts on the game," Brewer said. "Those types of conversations were invaluable. Of course, when he told me his opinion of the game, I would say something like, 'I couldn't agree more.'"

Most of the Canadian players agreed that after three games they were becoming accustomed to the spacing on the bigger, international ice surface. But where would Canada be without the timely play of Fleury, one of 11 Canadian players north of their 30th birthday, in the outing against the Czechs?

The smallest player in the Canadian lineup at 5'6" played a massive, and often overlooked, role in this tournament. After setting up Nieuwendyk for the tying goal, Fleury was at it again in the final seconds of the game. He got tangled up with Hasek and fell on the Czech goaltender. Czech defender Martin Skoula took a poke with his stick at Fleury while he was on his back. As he stood up Czech defenceman Roman Hamrlik skated in and gave the pint-sized Canadian forward a hard cross-check right below the No. 74 on the back of his jersey. Fleury was hurt. He was winded and prone on the ice. Hasek skated over to yell at the shift disturber. Once Fleury caught his breath, he made his way to the bench. There were 10 seconds left on the clock. Fleury's deed was done.

"It was obviously the last game of the round robin," Fleury explained. "As a guy who was brought in to provide a spark and some energy, the timing could not have been better. Basically, that was my role when we won the Stanley Cup in 1989 [with the Calgary

Flames]. I wasn't expected to light the world on fire points-wise, but I was expected to provide energy and momentum.

"I could feel the team was lacking in that department at that point in the Czech game. It was nothing more than that."

That he was on the Canadian team was a remarkable story in itself. His career was in a rut in 1999–00 at age 31. In his first year with the New York Rangers, he scored only 15 times. He had never scored fewer than 26 goals in his first 10 full NHL seasons.

Not many knew this at the time, but Fleury spent part of his summer in 2000 at a rehabilitation centre, dealing with his alcohol and drug abuse and demons from his youth. He appeared, on the surface, to be back on track in 2000–01. Through 62 games, he already had 30 goals and 74 points. He was fourth in league scoring.

In game No. 62 on Monday, February 26, 2001, Fleury set up Mark Messier for a first period goal in a 3-2 loss to the Ottawa Senators at home. This was a couple of weeks before the trade deadline. The Rangers had asked Fleury to waive the no-trade clause in his contract, but he refused the request.

He went out on the town after the game against Ottawa and later placed a call for help to Dr. David Lewis, one of the doctors with the NHLPA/NHL substance abuse program. Fleury voluntarily entered the in-patient program the next day. Messier told the New York reporters that he was surprised to learn of Fleury's setback and called the episode a "relapse."

The Rangers were nine points out of a playoff spot when Fleury's season ended. Fleury sent word through his agent a few days later that he was taking full responsibility for his actions. Lanny McDonald, who along with Gretzky was running Canada's entry for the World championship that spring, planned to invite Fleury to play for the national team. McDonald and Fleury were teammates and won a Stanley Cup together with the Flames in 1988–89.

Fleury spent five months in rehab, living in Santa Fe, New Mexico, in order to be close to a sponsor who made a difference, when his phone rang in late July. On the other end was Wayne Gretzky, calling to invite Fleury to the Canadian Olympic orientation camp in Calgary in early September.

"I couldn't believe it was Wayne on the phone," Fleury said. "He told me he had faith in me. It was a tremendous amount of motivation for me."

By the time Fleury arrived on the scene, midway through the Flames' 1988–89 season, Gretzky was in his first year with the Los Angeles Kings. So they avoided each other in the Battle of Alberta installments between Calgary and the Edmonton Oilers. But they did play against each other in the same conference for eight years. They also were teammates in the 1991 Canada Cup, 1996 World Cup of Hockey, and 1998 Olympics in Nagano.

"I was a Wayne Gretzky fan from the first time I saw him play on television," Fleury said. "To be around him and learn about what true leadership was all about, you can't buy that. He's a classy guy, the greatest guy of all time."

Fleury had been seen skating at the rink in his hometown of Russell, Manitoba, a few days before his first scheduled public appearance since his relapse on Monday, July 30, 2001, at the Pinebrook Golf Club in Calgary for his annual charity tournament. The event raised funds for Crohn's and Colitis Foundation research. He had suffered from the condition for most of his life.

Reporters from New York flew into Calgary for the event. But Fleury didn't provide details of what he was dealing with. He remarked he was proud he finally asked for help. Probably his biggest admission was his battle was day-to-day. Before he returned to Calgary for the orientation camp, Fleury found out he had a new teammate in Eric Lindros, who finally was dealt by the Philadelphia Flyers after he requested a trade.

In his return to New York, Fleury was inserted on a line with Lindros and Mike York when the 2001–02 season began. They led the Rangers offensively. All three played in the 2002 Olympics. York, however, was traded to Edmonton when he returned from his role on the United States team.

Fleury did his best to keep himself clean. But he was far from perfect. There were three concerning incidents. In San Jose in late December, he got into a hallway scuffle with the Sharks mascot, S.J. Sharkie, after Fleury had been tossed from the game.

A week later in Pittsburgh, he alarmed his teammates by going straight to the dressing room after his third consecutive slashing penalty with less than eight minutes remaining in the game. His excuse was he was dealing with an undisclosed family problem. It was the final outing of a six-game road trip in which he failed to score a point, checked in with 40 penalty minutes, and earned a plus-minus rating of minus-six.

Fleury then was fined $1,000 for flashing an obscene gesture following a 5–4 win on Long Island when Islanders fans chanted "Crackhead Theo" as he left the ice after scoring the game-winner, his second goal of the game.

Gretzky, however, kept his faith in Fleury. No. 99 had plenty of spies embedded with the Rangers to keep an eye on the right wing. Gretzky's former coach Glen Sather was the Rangers' GM, former Edmonton teammate Ron Low was the head coach, and former Oilers coach Ted Green was one of Low's assistants. But the biggest endorsement came from Messier.

"Part of the Theo story is I had just retired as a player," Gretzky said. "So I played against him. I've always said the one guy I hated to play against was Theo because he had a mean streak. Although he wasn't the biggest player, he had the biggest heart.

"He was a tremendous team player. Not everyone can be Mario or Sakic or Yzerman and play more than 18 minutes a game on a team like this. You need guys who are not going to play as much as they're used to with their teams in the NHL, but when they do play, they're going to make a contribution.

"I knew he was a pressure player. To me, Theo exemplifies Canadian hockey. He's an underdog. He overcame his size to play in the NHL. I just had so much respect for him as an athlete and he was a positive for us. I was so proud of him. Obviously, I was proud of everyone but extremely happy for Theo that the experience gave him a jumpstart at that point of his career."

Fleury paid back Gretzky's faith with his play, particularly late in the Czech game. He not only set up Nieuwendyk for the all-important, game-tying goal, but Fleury's dustup with Hasek, Skoula, and Hamrlik sent Gretzky into a postgame tizzy.

The early results produced harsh knocks against Gretzky. There were criticisms: Why didn't he give Patrick Roy a harder sell to play in Salt Lake City? Why wasn't Lemieux's health investigated more fully, especially with how well Joe Thornton had played since the Canadian roster had been announced in mid-December? Why wasn't Scotty Bowman the coach? There was speculation of dressing-room dissension. There was commentary that Canada's time was up.

Gretzky was frustrated. He was well aware of how well the Americans were performing. All he could imagine was another Miracle on Ice. After all, the last two times a Winter Olympics was held in the United States, the home side won men's hockey gold on both occasions. The U.S. were the victors in 1960 in Squaw Valley, California, riding the goalkeeping of Jack McCartan, and again in 1980 in Lake Placid, New York, under the inspired leadership of head coach Herb Brooks.

Brooks had returned to coach in 2002, and he was halfway to a successful reprisal in his role as a motivating force. The U.S. began with a 6–0 win against Finland, then tied Russia 2–2 and hammered Belarus 8–1 for a tournament-leading 16 goals through three games. They entered the playoff round as co-favourites along with Sweden.

The quarterfinal matchups were as follows: Czechs versus Russia; United States versus Germany; Sweden versus Belarus; Finland versus Canada.

"Up until we got to Salt Lake City, I was very comfortable with everything," Gretzky explained. "Steve [Tambellini], Kevin [Lowe], Lanny McDonald, the coaching staff, and Pat [Quinn] had put together a strong group. I was comfortable and confident.

"Then, with the loss to Sweden, the stress started to mount. Part of that was playing this tournament in the United States, where the U.S. won in 1960 and 1980. We didn't win in 1998 and then we started 2002 with a struggle, with a loss to Sweden, squeaked out a win over Germany, and then the tie with the Czechs.

"We were kind of puttering and the U.S. were flying. So more and more heat was coming my way. For that reason, I felt the pressure."

Gretzky also wasn't sleeping much. His lack of slumber was visible in his appearance. All these factors contributed to a contentious nine-minute, two-second press conference after the draw against the Czechs. Wearing a black turtleneck sweater, he took off his Hockey Canada blazer and hung it on the back of his chair before he took a seat behind the microphone. The Q and A started in mild fashion.

"There seem to be some greater possibilities for this team than there were 24 hours ago," Toronto-based radio reporter Howard Berger said.

"Well, first of all, the pressure and the expectation on our team is probably far greater than any other team in this tournament," Gretzky began. "Top that with the fact that we haven't won since the '50s makes it that much more difficult. We had a tough second period in Game 1. We had a very emotional game tonight. I thought we played really well, and now we're in a situation where we're going to play a team in Finland that plays very hard and we can kind of control our destiny.

"We played much better tonight with much more emotion and much more desperation. I thought we played very well."

The second question came from Dallas-based reporter Mike Heika. He asked Gretzky about the difference between Nieuwendyk's tying goal and if Canada lost 3–2. As explained before, a tie or loss didn't make a difference in Canada's seeding for the playoff round.

"You just," Gretzky said, stopping his thoughts to shrug his shoulders and looking agitated.

"Probably the biggest difference is what you guys write," Gretzky continued and then laughed when a few reporters chuckled. "The biggest thing is you want to go into any game on a high. We deserved a tie at worst tonight. I thought we played really well. Mario was tremendous. We're set up in a pretty good situation heading into Wednesday [quarterfinal day]."

Canadian television broadcaster Paul Romanuk had the microphone for the third question. He asked Gretzky why Canada usually requires three or four games to get rolling in tournaments like the Olympics and was it a case of a lack of respect by the Canadian NHLers for the international game.

"No, not at all," Gretzky said, shaking his head, moving his right index finger up to his right temple. "To a man, every player in [the Canadian dressing room] will tell you how great a player Hasek is. They will tell you how great [Mats] Sundin is, they'll tell you how great Jagr is. So we know they're good players."

And now the postgame session turned interesting.

"I don't think we dislike those other countries as much as they hate us. That's a fact. They don't like us, they want to see us fail, they love beating us. They may tell you something different, but believe me when you're on the ice, that's what they say. They don't like us. We gotta get that same feeling toward them.

"I mean, right now it's comical listening to things that are being said. It almost sickens my stomach to turn the TV on because I'm such a proud Canadian and such a fan of our game and very proud of all the players in the locker room, and it makes me ill to hear some of the things that are being said about us. Well, it's just not very good.

"And what's really annoying to me, in the '70s when we went through this whole thing about hooliganism and all that kind of stuff. If we would've did what they did tonight, it would have been a big story. I think the guy should be suspended for the rest of the tournament. If it was a Canadian player that did it, it would be a big story. But a Czech player did it, it's okay.

"I just don't understand it." Gretzky continued, referring to the Skoula spear and hard cross-check from Hamrlik on Fleury. "You guys saw it. If I'm wrong, I would tell you and I'd apologize. But one of the things we've gotta eliminate out of our game is that kind of stuff, and if a Canadian did it, it would be big news. But a Czech does it, and it's okay.

"And I don't understand it. There was a spear and a cross-check in the same play. I don't get it."

Gretzky then was asked if Canada's situation was similar to the New York Yankees being the most hated team in baseball.

"Probably," he said. "I mean, I heard a quote last night when we were tied 0–0 after the first period [against Germany].... It was like the Kansas City Royals being tied with the New York Yankees, two games to two. It was kind of ridiculous to me."

Lemieux's second goal of the game against the Czechs had to be reviewed because after making the save, Hasek rolled into the net with the puck. In the next question, Gretzky was asked, "You looked like you were on the edge of your seat reviewing that goal..."

"Well, it was clearly a goal," said Gretzky, cutting off the reporter. "There was nothing to review. I don't know what they were reviewing.

"They couldn't skate with us in the third period. They should have had four or five penalties, hooking, holding, tripping. We outplayed them in the third period. They talk about we're not a skating team and we couldn't move the puck, no finesse. That's crazy.

"We outskated them into the ground in the third period. There should have been four or five penalties, blatant penalties, and should have been two or three suspensions. Am I hot? Yeah I'm hot. Because I'm tired of people taking shots at Canadian hockey. When we do it, we're hooligans. But when Europeans do it, that's okay because they're not tough or they're not dirty. That's a crock of crap."

Globe and Mail reporter David Shoalts was up next. He relayed whispers around the rink that some of the veteran players were not happy with Pat Quinn's coaching style and lack of communication. Shoalts asked Gretzky if he felt the gossip was being spread by other countries.

"Absolutely. American propaganda," Gretzky said with a smile. The room erupted with laughter, although Gretzky wasn't joking.

Shoalts followed up with, "When you say American propaganda, who do you mean specifically? The American team or Herb Brooks?"

"No, no, not within the team," Gretzky said. "Absolutely not. Let me get that straight.

"Hey, if you want to talk about hockey, you talk about the Canadians. We're the biggest story down here. They're loving us not doing well. They're loving the start we've had. It's a big story for them. Now they have two Canadian stories, the figure skaters and the hockey team.

"It's such a crock of bull. We have great guys in our locker room. Nobody wants us to win but our own players. Our fans are loyal. People don't understand the pressure these guys are under and understand the b.s. our guys have to go through. And we're still here, we're still standing. We're proud players.

"Like I said, our country plays hard. We respect every team we play. We don't dislike them. Maybe sometimes when we dislike them, we play better. Like I said, if that was one of our players doing that, that would have been one of the first questions I would have been asked, 'Should he be suspended?' The guy should be suspended for the rest of the tournament. It's as simple as that. It's cowardly what happened. If a Canadian did it or an American player did it, we'd be hooligans."

Romanuk followed up with a question about the refereeing from Canadian Bill McCreary, who was regarded as the best in the NHL at the time. Gretzky was asked if he was "astounded" the episode involving Fleury was allowed to escalate under McCreary's watchful eye.

"I was more astounded that, you know what we say in hockey, paybacks are you-know-what," Gretzky said, shifting gears. "In the old days, you couldn't pay him back, so that's why we lost our tempers. So now they have to answer the fiddler in about a week, and paybacks are going to be awful tough, believe me. It's not going to be pretty. I wouldn't want to be in that Ranger-Islander game next week."

Fleury, of course, played for the Rangers. Hamrlik was with the New York Islanders at the time.

The final question of the press conference went to veteran Canadian broadcaster Bob McKenzie, who asked No. 99 to detail what he was so upset about with the Fleury-Hasek-Skoula-Harmrlik incident.

"Well, he cross-checked him in the back," Gretzky said. "He blatantly tried to hurt him. I don't understand it. But if it was a Canadian player who did it, the first question the European journalists asked me, 'Do you think he should be suspended or you guys are goons?'

"You know, I want to know why I wasn't asked that question. If it was my player who did it, that would have been the first question asked—should he be suspended? Are you disappointed in your team? Are you embarrassed by what happened?

"It happened to us. Our guy sucked it up. We played hard. We outskated them and we're still standing. Believe me, we've got a proud bunch in our locker room. I know the whole world wants us to lose, except for Canada and Canada fans and our players. And we'll be there. We'll be standing."

Gretzky was lauded in most media circles and by Canadian fans for standing up for his players. But he also was lambasted by a portion of columnists and commentators north and south of the 49th parallel. The critics called the press conference contrived. It was nothing more than a rant, a diatribe, a meltdown to take the heat off his players. The press conference was nothing more than a nine-minute whine session, a trait Gretzky haters accused him of in his playing days.

A headline in the *Edmonton Sun* called him "The Mad One." The *Calgary Sun* had another: "The Irate One." "Tension Getting to

Gretzky" was another in the *London Free Press*. "Great One or Great Whine," the *Ottawa Citizen* posited. "Suddenly, Gretzky's the Grate One" was another sharp headline in the *Kingston Whig-Standard*.

If you take the entire press conference, Gretzky was not out of control. He was not full of rage. These were not the words of a madman, a person at the end of his rope. He was passionate. At times, he was indignant. But this was far from a rant or diatribe as many described the scene.

Sure, you can take a sound bite from Gretzky's time behind the microphone or a couple of the responses for a newspaper column to sensationalize his postgame remarks. He did veer from being annoyed to apoplectic a few times. But Gretzky spoke from the heart. His responses weren't eloquent, but his words hit the mark.

Immediately, people equated Gretzky's turn at the mic to Phil Esposito's passionate plea to Canadians midway through the Summit Series, 30 years earlier. After Game 4 in Vancouver, a 5–3 loss to the Soviet Union to put Canada behind with only one win, two losses, and a tie, Esposito conducted an interview with reporter Johnny Esaw after Team Canada was booed off the ice.

"To the people across Canada, we tried, we gave it our best, and to the people that boo us, geez, I'm really, all of us guys are really disheartened and we're disillusioned, and we're disappointed at some of the people," Esposito said. "We cannot believe the bad press we've got, the booing we've gotten in our own buildings.

"I'm really disappointed. I am completely disappointed. I cannot believe it. Some of our guys are really, really down in the dumps. We know, we're trying like hell. I mean, we're doing the best we can, and they got a good team, and let's face facts. But it doesn't mean that we're not giving it our 150 per cent, because we certainly are.

"I mean, every one of us guys, 35 guys that came out and played for Team Canada. We did it because we love our country, and not for any other reason, no other reason. They can throw the money, uh, for the pension fund out the window. They can throw anything they want out the window. We came because we love Canada. And even though we play in the United States, and we earn money in the United States, Canada is still our home, and that's the only reason we come. And I don't think it's fair that we should be booed."

Gretzky maintains, then and now, his press conference that night wasn't contrived. He was upset with what he witnessed at the game and simply answered the questions. He did admit after the gold medal game to reporters that he channelled his inner Glen Sather to take the heat off his players, but there were no regrets, not now nor the day after.

"I learned that from Glen Sather. You have to stand up and take responsibility," Gretzky said of his former Edmonton Oilers coach and GM.

"I just felt on Monday that our team, behind the scenes, we were taking so much criticism, I felt like we weren't comfortable and relaxed.

"I just thought, *Okay, let me take some heat off these guys.* I did and then I didn't sleep for five days."

"I was trying to protect our hockey team and I was saying it out of passion for Canada. I have no regrets about what I said. I said there was a penalty and it was blatant. I said they love to beat us and that there's no better feeling for them than beating the Canadian hockey team. Why should I have regrets about saying that?"

Gretzky claimed he heard too many rumours about his team and the whispers got to him. One piece of gossip, he said, was Lemieux was too hurt and was going home.

Canadian goalie Curtis Joseph was the fall guy in the tournament opener as his teammates started slowly with a 5–2 defeat. His Toronto Maple Leafs teammate Mats Sundin scored twice for Sweden against Canada.

A couple days after his passionate rant, Gretzky sat nervously watching his team stretch before their do-or-die quarterfinal round game against Finland.

Canadian goalie Martin Brodeur saved his best for the final three games against Finland, Belarus, and the United States, keeping his eye on the prize with 62 saves on 66 shots for a .939 save percentage.

Canadian captain Mario Lemieux sets up defenceman Scott Niedermayer to put Canada ahead 3–1 against Belarus to advance to the final. Eric Lindros also scored his team's sixth goal as seven different Canadians scored in the 7–1 semifinal victory.

Canada fell behind 1–0 early in the gold medal final against the United States. But Paul Kariya scored to tie the game when Mario Lemieux allowed Chris Pronger's pass to slip through his legs to Kariya for a dandy goal.

Rugged Canadian forward Ryan Smyth was one of the inspiring stories on the Canadian roster. He suffered a broken ankle weeks before Gretzky was to name the Canadian team, but Smyth overcame the pain and played a pivotal role.

Jarome Iginla was a late invite to Canada's summer camp because of an injury to Simon Gagne. Iginla made the most of his opportunity, smartly starting the season with the Calgary Flames and making the team. Here, he scored Canada's 2–1 goal in the gold medal final, his first of two goals in the final.

Canadian forward Joe Sakic was the game's all-around best player by the time Salt Lake City rolled around. He had won his second Stanley Cup eight months earlier with the Colorado Avalanche, as well as winning the 2000-01 Hart Trophy and being named the 2002 Olympic tournament MVP. This was his second of two goals in the final and the tournament's last goal.

Joe Sakic, Jarome Iginla, and Simon Gagne were the most dependable line for Canada. The three combined to score Canada's final four goals in the 5-2 gold medal final win.

The relief and emotion were immediately evident as Canada ended a 50-year gold medal drought in men's Olympic hockey.

Canadian forward Theo Fleury's career was in jeopardy as he was dealing with substance abuse demons the summer before the Games. Executive director Wayne Gretzky took a chance on the fiery Fleury, and the diminutive forward came up big for Canada.

After Team Canada's Olympic victory, head coach Pat Quinn (back row, fifth from left) pulled his daughter Kalli (right of Quinn) onto the ice for the celebratory team photo.

"That one got in my craw," Gretzky said. "Every time I walked into the arena, it was a different story. Finally, I'd had enough of it."

Gretzky's commentary produced mixed reaction among the Canadian players. Many of them weren't aware of his emotional presser until the following morning. But they all appreciated Gretzky putting his emotions on public display.

"We didn't know exactly what happened until later," Ryan Smyth said. "I remember seeing him come into our room and you could see he was ticked off. There is no more passionate guy than Gretz. His passion allowed us to survive."

Adam Foote added, "For me, it was nothing. But it was smart. [Gretzky] was trying to get us a fair shake with the refs. He also was trying to take the heat off us."

Rob Blake said, "He took away the distractions for us. We were sheltered from what was going on out there around the games and back in Canada. Don't forget there was no social media like there is now. But he took it upon himself to take the heat. I do think it calmed us down."

Steve Yzerman had a slightly different take.

"For us, it's really not an issue at all," the Red Wings captain told a scrum of reporters the next day. "It's not something we're talking about. We're wrapped in getting ready to play, so we're not really concerned with people's reaction."

The man in the middle of the whole hullabaloo, Fleury, appreciated Gretzky standing up for him and the team.

"I would say the majority of the guys didn't know about Wayne's rant until later because we were so isolated," Fleury said. "There was no panic with us, but after the game against the Czechs it was almost like a switch had been turned on. Our focus was on another level."

Kevin Lowe took partial blame for getting Gretzky amped up. Most mornings in Salt Lake City, Gretzky and his father, Walter, would have breakfast at a Denny's restaurant near his downtown accommodations. Lowe and others would often join them.

The Blackberry mobile device had been introduced and Lowe had one in his possession. He could access the internet and he kept Gretzky abreast of what was being written about the Canadian team across North America.

"I could get all the media stories," Lowe said. "When things weren't going well, there were lots of stories about Canada and speculation as to why we weren't playing well. As I was reading Wayne these stories, he was getting hot. So it was no surprise he did what he did.

"There was a buildup. It wasn't just one thing. We lost to Sweden. We didn't play well against Germany and then there was what happened in the Czech game.

"Wayne, as a player, was always that passionate. As the best player on the ice, there always was that calmness about him. But there were times he could blow a gasket. It was neat to see because as a teammate it was sort of like, 'Wow, he is human.'"

Gretzky's thoughts on his passion play all these years later is interesting. He summarizes it as an attempt to defend his team as a proud Canadian.

"It came out of the blue," Gretzky said. "It definitely was not preplanned. Part of why it came out was sitting around throughout the previous few days and watching the U.S. coverage. We were getting criticized, things like, 'Was the Canadian team going to show up?' Or, 'Was it overrated?' etc., etc.

"We always had this image of being tough and sometimes excessively tough. But it's never been brought to the forefront that other countries can be tough against us. So when the cross-check happened, it wasn't anything personal. I just really believed the consequences would have been different if our player delivered the cross-check.

"So sitting there, one thing led to another. I knew it was about defending our country, how proud Canadians are and how badly we wanted to win a gold medal. I was disappointed over years and years of not getting that Olympic gold medal and it happened quick.

"I remember going back to the downtown apartment I was staying at and seeing the reaction, and then thinking, 'Oh my gosh, this wasn't what I anticipated.'"

There was one final piece of backlash he had not anticipated. When Gretzky states that he has no regrets about his so-called rant, that's not entirely true. After another session with reporters on the off day, in between the Czech outing and the quarterfinal matchup against Finland, there was somebody waiting for him in the parking lot near the Canadian team bus. It was referee Bill McCreary.

The personable McCreary enjoyed a pristine reputation with NHL players. In fact, when the gold medal game arrived a few days later, the U.S. players demanded McCreary officiate the championship affair even though he was a Canadian, born and raised in Guelph, Ontario.

An IIHF rule prohibited a referee from officiating a gold medal game if his country was involved. McCreary's inclusion in the 2002 final changed all that and to this day officials from other countries thank him for the modification.

McCreary had taken a call from his wife, Mary Ann, the day after Gretzky's postgame presser. The McCrearys' 12-year-old daughter, Melissa, was mocked and teased by her classmates at St. Paul Elementary School back in Guelph. Mary Ann was upset. Melissa was upset. Her classmates had labeled her dad a cheater.

One of McCreary's traits as an official was his tremendous communication skills with the players during the heat of a game. So he decided the best course of action would be to meet with Gretzky to let him know what had happened. McCreary glanced at the practice schedule that day, found out the time Canada had slated for its on-ice session, and waited outside the rink for Gretzky.

"I asked to speak to him for a moment," McCreary said. "I told him what had happened. I told him his voice carried so much weight. He didn't miss a beat. He offered to phone my daughter immediately to apologize and phone the kids at the school.

"His offer took me aback so quickly because I thought we were going to have a confrontation, more than anything. I was ready for that. He probably wasn't ready for me. But his professionalism was amazing."

McCreary wanted to make sure he never accused Gretzky of calling him a cheater.

"He didn't use the word 'cheat' or 'cheater,'" said McCreary, a Hockey Hall of Fame inductee in 2014, who also refereed the 1998 and 2010 Olympic gold medal games. "But he wasn't happy with my work. He brought that specific play to the attention of the media.

"I just think Wayne was hot with the criticism in the media about the way some of the players had been playing, and he felt that Canada had been on the wrong end of some of the calls. He brought that up with the non-call on Theo.

"It was a very aggressive game. There was a lot going on. I don't know how many penalties were called, but not a lot. There was no question when you have a competitive guy like Theo, things like that happen. I loved watching him play. He's a small man in terms of stature in the game but he played much bigger than most people within the game."

For his part, Gretzky still feels horrible about the angst his words inadvertently caused the McCrearys.

"I felt so bad," Gretzky said. "It wasn't him I meant to single out. He mentioned to me that kids in his daughter's school were picking on her. So I offered to call the school and talk to the kids to let them know it wasn't the referee's fault.

"I don't think I ever felt that bad after that. It wasn't personal. I was just trying to defend our team and our country. You get so emotional."

There were a pair of happy endings to this episode. Not only did Gretzky exhibit remorse and grace with McCreary, but the referee was also at his best once again in the gold medal game a few days later.

There were no complaints from either side. In fact, if you review a video of the gold medal match, amid the on-ice mayhem after the game, Canadian head coach Pat Quinn can be seen seeking out McCreary to shake his hand. As the United States team waited for the medal ceremony, 13 players wearing the Stars and Stripes shook the referee's hand.

"As far as I was concerned, there were 40 guys playing who I had refereed in the NHL before," McCreary said. "One team was in red and white and the other team was in blue and white."

CHAPTER 7

Big Break
from Belarus

Queried years later as to whether he felt his passionate plea following the Czech game was the turning point for Canada's journey in Salt Lake City, Wayne Gretzky answered with an emphatic "no." Instead, he was quick to volunteer that Theo Fleury setting up Joe Nieuwendyk for the late game-tying goal against the Czechs was what changed the course for the Canadian team.

"If we don't score that goal, there would have been all kinds of doubt in the dressing room," Gretzky said. "We had played so well in that game. We outplayed them. That goal gave us a good feeling going into the next game against the Finns."

Gretzky and Canada knew Finland would provide the most difficult test yet. Finland didn't start out well in Salt Lake City. But after a 6–0 loss to the United States, the Finns rebounded with an 8–1 victory against Belarus and 3–1 win against their most ardent rival, Russia. Whenever Finland defeated its next-door neighbours from Russia, it was a massive deal for the Scandinavian country.

It should be noted the Finns were an inspired bunch in Salt Lake City. They were without one of their best players, their leader, Saku Koivu. He pushed Finland to a surprise world championship title in 1995. He was only 20 at the time and had yet to suit up for his first NHL game with the Montreal Canadiens.

Now 27, and in the prime of his career, Koivu arrived back in town in early September 2001 for Canadiens' training camp. He didn't feel right. Sure enough, after undergoing a series of tests, the news was bad. He was diagnosed with stomach cancer. Mario Lemieux, a cancer survivor himself, was among several players to contact the Montreal captain to pick up his spirits.

Koivu was going to travel to Salt Lake City to be around and cheer on his fellow countrymen. But he decided to stay home. His treatment went as well as could be expected. His cancer was in remission. A comeback was on his mind. He wanted to return to action in time for the playoffs. (He did return for the final three regular season games and helped the Canadiens advance to the second round of the playoffs.)

The Finns played a game similar to the Germans. Both teams incorporated a passive forecheck, defence-first system. The Finns often strung five players along the blue line, hoping to create a turnover. They preferred low-scoring defensive struggles.

"We knew this was going to be a hard, hard game," Canadian assistant coach Ken Hitchcock said. "It was going to be a real battle because it had the potential to be so frustrating. They gave up the forecheck and waited for us to make mistakes.

"We needed to be patient. To ask the most skilled players in the world like we had to play a dump and chase game is difficult, a real challenge."

Finland was led offensively by Teemu Selanne. Canadian head coach Pat Quinn wanted to limit Selanne's impact on the game. So the line that played such a significant part in the Czech game—Fleury, Nieuwendyk, and Michael Peca—received the assignment of keeping Selanne in check. Particularly, Peca was to shadow the player known as the Finnish Flash.

Selanne was good friends with Paul Kariya. The two played together for the Anaheim Ducks for parts of six seasons. So did Kariya offer any secrets to Peca on how to cover Selanne?

"Michael didn't need any help from me," Kariya said with a chuckle. "Nobody ever asked me for defensive pointers. So the answer is no. He obviously figured it out."

Peca had become quite the story for Canada. A tenacious two-way player, he won the Frank J. Selke Trophy in 1996–97 as the NHL's best defensive forward and helped the Buffalo Sabres advance to the 1998–99 Stanley Cup against the Hitchcock-coached Dallas Stars. There was no doubt about Peca's talent. But the year before the Olympics, like Eric Lindros, he missed the entire season because of a contract dispute with the Sabres. Lindros sat out after he requested a trade from the Philadelphia Flyers.

To stay in shape, Peca rented an hour of ice time five days a week at the Northtown Center in suburban Buffalo, New York. Phil Christ, a friend, tagged along. He bravely strapped on the pads to allow Peca to work on his shot. Peca was driven. He followed a routine in which all his drills were performed at an up-tempo pace for 30 to 40 seconds, the same length of time for most shifts in the NHL.

The Sabres occasionally practiced at Northtown, too. It led to some awkward moments, crossing paths with some of his former teammates. Peca remarked that Buffalo head coach Lindy Ruff always was there with an encouraging word.

"He would pull me into a broom closet to chat," Peca recalled. "He kept my spirits up."

There were a couple of times Peca gave his buddy Phil Christ a respite that season. In the hopes of staying sharp, Peca decided to play for Canada at the 2000 Spengler Cup between Christmas and New Years in Davos, Switzerland, and again for Canada at the 2001 World championship in Germany. However, both tournaments did not go as well as expected for the out-of-work talent.

In Davos, a rusty Peca suffered a groin injury on his first shift. The strain was severe enough to knock him out of the rest of the tournament. In Germany, Peca was named Canada's captain. He looked nothing like a player who hadn't performed in a meaningful game in a year. Peca was a physical force. He helped Canada begin with three consecutive wins, including a masterful performance in a 5–1 win against Russia. Peca scored a goal and an assist and completely shut down Alexei Yashin to help Canada's cause in a big way.

But one of his monster bodychecks on a Russian defender left Peca with a fractured left cheekbone. He finished the game despite the serious injury. But his tournament was over. Canada never recovered, losing 4–3 in overtime to the United States in the quarterfinals. Peca, however, made enough of an impression on Gretzky and the management team to warrant an invitation to the orientation camp in Calgary.

Quinn always liked Peca's play. He had drafted Peca in the second round in 1992 for Vancouver. Peca was one of the Canucks' black aces (spare players) in their run to the 1993–94 Stanley Cup Final, but he was traded to Buffalo after the 1994–95 season.

Peca found a new home in the summer of 2001, when the Sabres finally dealt him to the New York Islanders. He made life easy for the Canadian Olympic management team to find a roster spot for him. Peca had scored seven times and checked in with 24 points in the 29 games before Canada's roster was named. He also was healthy and had re-established himself as one of the most diligent forwards in the game. In fact, he would win his second Selke Trophy for the 2001–02 season.

He fit nicely between Nieuwendyk and Fleury as Canada's shut-down line. There was the odd occasion Brendan Shanahan would take a shift on the line, but for the most part this trio stuck together for the entire 2002 Olympic tournament. The offensive units of Joe Sakic between Simon Gagne and Jarome Iginla was discovered in the Germany game. The Lemieux, Steve Yzerman, and Paul Kariya three-some was instituted for the match against the Czechs. Eric Lindros with Ryan Smyth and Owen Nolan would enjoy their best game in the gold medal final.

"I think we came together rather easily because we all played a similar style, a simple game," Peca said. "At that point in our careers we were each 200-foot players."

The entire Canadian team enjoyed a patient and responsible 200-foot game against Finland. Canada outshot Finland 34–19 and only a solid effort from Finnish goalie Jani Hurme, who played that season for Canadian assistant coach Jacques Martin and the Ottawa Senators, prohibited the game from being more lopsided. Hurme made 14 saves in the first period to keep the Finns close. They only were behind 1–0 until late in the second period.

Sakic floated a backhand for an early Canadian lead, three minutes in. Lemieux and Yzerman combined on a nifty give-and-go goal with less than five minutes remaining in the second period when Yzerman received a pass from Lemieux on the edge of the crease and the Red Wings captain lifted a shot up over Hurme.

But Canada's two-goal lead lasted only 20 seconds. Niklas Hagman, whose father, Matti, was a teammate of Gretzky and Kevin Lowe with the Edmonton Oilers, stuffed in a goal from the side of Canadian goalie Martin Brodeur. But the Canadians did not panic and methodically closed the deal on the 2–1 victory with a goalless final 20 minutes.

There only was one close call in the third period. Canadian defenceman Ed Jovanovski was whistled for a boarding penalty at the 6:10 mark. Peca and the Canadian penalty killers were stingy. The only chance Finland produced was a setup from Selanne to Sami Kapanen, whose shot slid wide of the mark.

About the only hitch in the game for Canada was Shanahan suffered a fractured right thumb after taking a slash during his first shift. But he didn't miss any time in the game against Finland or the rest of the tournament.

"The whole group was so calm," said Peca, referring to his Canadian teammates. "You think about players like Mario, Steve Yzerman, Joe Sakic, Al MacInnis, Rob Blake, and Joe Nieuwendyk, they have seen so much and been through so much.

"I often said that when a coach panics, the players panic. But those guys were in so much control. Mario, especially, he was such a rock and it just trickled down."

The Canada-Finland game was the last of the four quarterfinal games. The outcome was a perfect ending to what had been a favourable day for the Canadians. In the first quarterfinal, Canada's opening-day nemesis, Sweden, was stunned by Belarus 4–3. Dominik Hasek and the Czech Republic were knocked out by Russia 1–0 and the host United States had an easy time with a 5–0 advantage against Germany for the U.S.'s second shutout of the tournament. The Americans had now outscored the opposition by a combined 21–3 in four outings.

While the Russian-Czech game was considered a toss-up, the Canadians didn't mind seeing the prospects of meeting Hasek in the gold medal final go by the wayside. But watching Belarus take out Sweden was a shocker. Canada expected to meet Sweden again in the semifinals.

After Nik Lidstrom put Sweden in front early, Belarus overcame the deficit to take a 2–1 lead midway through the first period and enjoyed a 3–2 advantage, 2:47 into the final frame. Mats Sundin tied the game for a third time with a little more than 12 minutes remaining.

Surely Sweden would pull this one out with the firepower of players like Sundin, Daniel Alfredsson, Markus Naslund, and Lidstrom. But they huffed and puffed and couldn't put any more pucks past Mezin the Magnificent as Belarus goalkeeper Andrei Mezin became known on that day. He wound up stopping 44 Swedish shots.

The 27-year-old Mezin was raised in Minsk and as a teenager played two seasons of tier II junior hockey with the Brockville Braves, near the Canadian capital of Ottawa.

The 5'11", 170-pound Mezin had been peppered throughout the tournament. He entered the game against Sweden with a less-than-average .857 save percentage after a pair of blowout 8–1 losses to the United States and Finland.

The 6–4 defeat against Russia to open the tournament seemed like a victory for Belarus, a former Soviet state that at the time only had 820 registered hockey players and six rinks. Belarus had one NHLer in the lineup in defenceman Ruslan Salei, a teammate of Kariya in Anaheim. Another, Vladimir Tsyplakov, was playing in Russia, but he was a former member of the Los Angeles Kings and Buffalo. He actually played 11 games with Wayne Gretzky on the 1995–96 Kings.

Belarus also had a Kovalev, but an Andrei Kovalev, not the Russian Olympian Alexei Kovalev, who won a Stanley Cup with the New York Rangers and was Lemieux's teammate in Pittsburgh at the time. Andrei Kovalev put Belarus ahead 3–2 early in the third period with an unassisted goal after picking off a pass from Swedish defenceman Mattias Ohlund. With the game tied at 3–3, defenceman

Vladimir Kopat drifted a harmless shot from just inside the centre line. The 90-footer was directed at the head of the Swedish goalie Tommy Salo. The Oilers goalie, who defeated Canada in the 1994 Olympic gold medal shootout, tried to catch the puck. He got a piece, but the puck had enough momentum to squeeze between the goalie's catching glove and head and rolled down his back and into the goal. Swedish defenceman Kenny Jonsson made a diving effort to halt the puck's progress, but it was too late. Alfredsson and Sundin coasted toward the Sweden goal in disbelief.

The score clock read 17:36. Back in 2002, the time in a period in the international game counted up, not down. There was 2:24 remaining. The pro-Belarus crowd was going bonkers. The Swedes mustered only one good offensive opportunity after Kopat's goal. But Mezin turned aside Niklas Sundstrom's shot from in close with 67 seconds remaining.

The unlikely result was likened to the United States' Miracle on Ice upset over the Soviet Union at the 1980 Olympics in Lake Placid, New York. In fact, as Belarus broke bread during a team meal the night before, they discussed the Miracle on Ice.

"For us it is [the same]," Salei said after the game. "It's that big."

"Hockey is a team game," Mezin added. "It is a lucky game sometimes."

Canada caught a huge break with the shocking upset. Salo and the Swedes, in the meantime, were in for a rough few days. Swedish daily newspaper *Svenska Dagbladet* designed a fake stamp with a picture of goalie Tommy Salo covering his face mask as the puck bounced off his head and into the net. The postmark caption read: "Salt Lake City 2002—Fiasco." This was in jest because of the 1994 stamp that honoured Forsberg's shootout goal in the Olympic gold medal final against Canada, when Salo was one of the heroes. Another newspaper, *Aftonbladet*, published a headline "The Day of Shame," while another, *Expressen*, printed photos of each player with their NHL salary underneath. The story was accompanied by the headline, "Guilty: They Betrayed Their Country."

"Of course, it's tough, it's always going to be tough, but I'm going to get over it," Salo told reporters when he arrived back in Edmonton. "I'm still thinking about it. It's my toughest time ever, but when I go back on the ice, I'm not going to think about it."

Salo took plenty of supportive phone calls after the game, including one from Canadian defenceman Eric Brewer and another from assistant GM Kevin Lowe.

Mezin instantly became the darling of the men's hockey tournament. He joked with reporters on the day in between the win against Sweden and the semifinal against Canada that he celebrated only with two beers because he was exhausted and needed some sleep.

Canada could not afford to take Belarus lightly, especially if Mezin was going to put forth another all-world effort. The Canadians had concerns of their own. Even though they had outshot the opposition 137–81 in their four outings, they had scored only 10 times. Sakic and Lemieux were feeling it with two goals apiece. But capable goal scorers like Eric Lindros, Jarome Iginla, Brendan Shanahan, and Simon Gagne were yet to check in with a goal.

The offence needed a boost, but now it appeared they would have their hands full with another hot goalie in Mezin.

"It's such a short tournament," Canadian defenceman Rob Blake said. "The frustration can build if you don't score early."

The Canadians said all the right things after their light 45-minute skate in preparation for the Belarus game. Most of the team went for a quick bite and hurried back to the E Center to cheer on the Canadian women's team in its late-afternoon gold medal clash with the rival United States. Nobody wanted to leave because the women's finale turned out to be another classic. What the Canadian men witnessed lifted their spirits.

The U.S. were favoured to repeat. They celebrated eight wins in a row in tune-up games against Canada before arriving in Salt Lake City. But the Canadian women struck first on a goal from Caroline Ouellette. All of a sudden they were feeling good about their chances to avenge the disappointment of Nagano four years earlier.

Kathryn King, however, tied the game early in the second period with a power-play goal. This goal came while Canadian defender Becky Kellar was in the penalty box for tripping. It was the fifth of eight consecutive penalties called on Canada by American referee Stacey Livingston. Even members of the Canadian men's team, some sitting in the last row in the corner of the building, others were standing behind them, jeered the decisions made by the official. But the Canadian women pressed on and persevered.

Hayley Wickenheiser, the best women's player in the world, pushed Canada out to a 2–1 lead 2:11 after King's goal. Jayna Hefford scored to provide a two-goal bulge for the underdogs.

The U.S. pulled to within a goal with another power-play marker with less than four minutes remaining in the third period. It was their 11th power-play opportunity, compared to just four for Canada in the game. But Canadian goalie Kim St. Pierre shut the door in the final 3:33. As the women celebrated their emotional victory, Martin Brodeur and the men's team applauded from the stands.

Canadian head coach Pat Quinn was particularly moved by what the women accomplished. He made his way down to the Canadian women's bench after the game with tears in his eyes, saying, "They never lost their poise. It was a magnificent victory."

"It's one of my favourite moments from that Olympics in Salt Lake City, to see him in tears," Wickenheiser recalled. "He told me later that the women inspired the men."

The women's victory dominated the conversation that evening at the Canadian men's team dinner in a private room at a steakhouse on the outskirts of town. But before the players returned to the Olympic Village, Quinn sent them on their way with a message: play like the women. What he meant by that was to perform with a hefty dose of controlled emotion.

"It can be one of our biggest enemies and one our best friends," Quinn explained to reporters after the game against Belarus. "I saw in two days how emotion can work for you and against you. The Swedish team, in my opinion the best team here, started to lose concentration [against Belarus]. They started making defensive mistakes, slamming gates, barking at each other. They lost their focus.

"Then I watched our [women's] team. I've never seen homerism like this in all my life [with the one-sided refereeing]. But they never lost their poise. It was amazing. You lose your poise, you give in to the circumstances, that's what loses it. You lose your focus and we spoke about that in our meeting."

At the end of the steak dinner, dessert had arrived. It was Ryan Smyth's 26th birthday. It was the perfect way to celebrate the women's inspiring win.

"The women set the stage for us men," said Smyth, who added there wasn't a hint of overconfidence going into the semifinal against Belarus the following afternoon.

"We learned our lesson earlier in the tournament with the first two games. We weren't going to take anyone lightly. Our mind-set was to take care of business one game at a time after those first two games."

The Canadians did take care of business against Belarus, and how. But the victory didn't come without an early scare. After Yzerman put Canada ahead 1–0 on the seventh shift of the game, Salei tied up the proceedings later in the opening period to provide for an anxious moment or two before Eric Brewer restored the Canadian lead prior to the intermission.

Canada would increase its lead to 4–1 by the end of 40 minutes and score three more times in the final period to toast a 7–1 rout. Mezin was bombarded early and often. He was pulled after the fourth goal, already having faced 27 shots with the game just past the midway mark. Canada outshot Belarus by a whopping 51–14 advantage.

The Canadians had to wait around to see which team they would face in the gold medal final, Russia or the U.S. The home side jumped out to a 3–0 lead after two periods, but goals from Kovalev and Vladimir Malakhov early in the third period made for a nervous final 16 minutes. The U.S., however, hung on for a 3–2 victory to set up an all–North America final.

"We knew coming in this can be an awful albatross," Quinn said about Canada's bid to end the 50-year drought. "We're carrying the hopes of the nation. Somehow in Canada, we expect more. I don't know if we'll win, but we're there [in the gold medal final]. We plan on it."

The good news for Quinn's side was they snapped out of their offensive slump. The Lemieux-Kariya-Yzerman line provided four goals, with Yzerman scoring first, and the Red Wings captain then set up Brewer for the go-ahead second goal. Kariya and Lemieux combined to put Scott Niedermayer in position for a power-play goal. Kariya then made it 4–1.

Gagne, while Canada was shorthanded, scored another on a nifty play from Peca. Lindros and Iginla would complete the scoring for

Canada as each collected their first goals of the tournament. While the offence from Gagne and Iginla was a harbinger of what was to come in the gold medal match, the goals from Lindros and Niedermayer were welcome tallies.

By the time Niedermayer concluded his career, he would skate off into the sunset as one of the most decorated players in hockey history. He was known for his skating and passing and quiet leadership.

"My quiet personality is great to have in certain situations, not so good in other situations when you need a little emotion," Niedermayer confessed. "There are times when you need that emotion, but that's my personality."

Niedermayer was 28 years old when he arrived in Salt Lake City. He was already a world junior winner with Canada in 1991 and a Memorial Cup champion. He was named tournament MVP with the 1991–92 Kamloops Blazers and was a two-time Stanley Cup title-holder with the New Jersey Devils in 1994–95 as well as 1999–2000. He played for Canada at the 1996 World Cup of Hockey but was inexplicably left off the roster for the 1998 Olympics.

Despite all these accolades and accomplishments, Niedermayer felt like a kid skating alongside all the talent on the Canadian team.

"It was such a thrill to play with a guy like Mario Lemieux," Niedermayer said. Lemieux opted not to play for Canada in 1996. "I had so much respect for his skill and his talent.

"Then growing up in Cranbrook, [British Columbia], I can't remember how old I was, but I remember seeing on the back of Steve Yzerman's hockey card that his birthplace was Cranbrook. That was such a highlight for me as a kid. So playing with him in Salt Lake City was a thrill."

After the thrill of winning in Salt Lake City, Niedermayer was far from done when it came to claiming championships and individual honours. In a 16-month stretch, he would celebrate a third Stanley Cup with the 2002–03 Devils, the 2003–04 Norris Trophy as the NHL's top defenceman, a win at the 2004 World Championship in May, and the World Cup of Hockey title in September 2004. He also scored the championship-clinching goal against Finland in the World Cup.

The 2004 World Championship in Prague, Czech Republic, was especially memorable. The title meant Niedermayer became the 14th athlete in history to join the Triple Gold Club as a hockey player who won a Stanley Cup, world championship, and Olympic gold in a career. But what made the world championship victory especially cool was he won the coveted crown alongside his brother, Rob, who was 16 months younger.

It was tough on their parents, Carol and Bob, in the spring of 2003 when Scott's Devils prevailed over Rob and the Anaheim Ducks in a hard-fought seven-game series. But the pair had so much fun performing together in Prague that when Scott became a free agent in 2005, he signed with Anaheim to play with Rob in the NHL. In their second season together, they won the Stanley Cup with Chris Pronger. Scott won the Conn Smythe Trophy as MVP. Rob played on a shutdown line with Travis Moen and Sami Pahlsson that also was a significant factor for the winning side.

A knee injury prohibited Scott Niedermayer from participating in the 2006 Olympics in Turin, Italy, but he returned for his last international hurrah in Vancouver, British Columbia, in 2010. Niedermayer was named team captain and Canada won gold.

"Salt Lake City was my first kick at the can in the Olympics," said Scott, later inducted into the Canadian Sports and Hockey Halls of Fame. "We stuck together early in the tournament when we needed time to mesh. I don't remember any finger pointing or anybody making any excuses.

"The coaches and the management team kept us focused on what we were there to do. We also had some great leaders who kept a level head and a quiet confidence among the group that we'd be okay.

"I always tell people that Salt Lake City felt more like a business trip. We were there to get a job done. But don't get me wrong, we were all well aware it had been 50 years."

While good times seemed to follow Niedermayer around, the same cannot be said about Lindros. A massive talent with his size and skill, Lindros was trailed by turmoil, heartbreak, and a long list of injuries. He battled a number of concussions, a collapsed lung, and knee problems on the physical side. On the mental side, he dealt with the disappointment of being swept by Yzerman and the Red Wings in the 1996–97 Stanley Cup Final and the despair of the 1998 Olympics.

Bobby Clarke, the leader of the management team in 1998, remarked that it was a mistake to have named Lindros the captain of the Canadian Olympic team because Gretzky was on the team and most of the other players looked to the Great One for leadership. Some of the players from that team agreed this still was Gretzky's team, and because he was neglected for the captain role, the tournament didn't go as smoothly as expected.

"I never played on a team with Mario," Lindros said when asked why the 2002 team won and the 1998 edition whiffed. "He was a huge factor for us. We also didn't have Kariya in 1998 and Joe Sakic was hurt and missed the final. Those were big factors."

Another big factor was the way the 1998 and 2002 Olympic tournaments played out. Canada was excellent early on and then hit a wall named Dominik Hasek in the semifinals in 1998. Four years later, the

Canadians struggled and then pulled themselves together in the nick of time.

"We didn't have our act together early in Salt Lake City," Lindros said. "We found our way, whereas we didn't lose a period until the Czech game in 1998. That pretty much sums up the difference.

"We also weren't prepared for the shootout. I'm not pointing the finger at anybody. The shootout was new to us culturally and we weren't ready for it. The shooters weren't prepared, neither were the coaches and goaltenders. Look at the difference now. We practiced shootouts at the end of practices in 2002 and now every team does it in the NHL every day since the shootout was adopted [in 2005]."

Like Peca, Lindros was invited to the orientation camp in Calgary after having sat out the entire 2000–01 season. But unlike Peca, Lindros decided against playing for Canada in the Spengler Cup and world championship. The big man was coming off a troubled time in his career. He was lambasted by Boston Bruins giant defenceman Hal Gill in a game on March 4, 2000. Lindros played in four more outings before he was diagnosed with a third concussion that season.

He criticized the team, its training staff, and its physicians for allowing him to play four games after he suffered the head injury. The old-school Clarke, the Flyers general manager, was incensed at what he perceived as insubordination on Lindros' part. Clarke demanded an apology. In the meantime, he stripped Lindros of the team captaincy.

Lindros returned to action 10 weeks later in time for Game 6 of the East final against Brodeur, Niedermayer, and the Devils. Lindros scored the lone goal in Philadelphia's 2–1 loss to set up a seventh and deciding game. In Game 7, midway through the first period, Lindros cut across the Devils blue line with his head down and New Jersey defencemen Scott Stevens caught the Flyers forward with a devastating open-ice hit.

Lindros was knocked unconscious and had to be helped off the ice. A week later, as the Devils were marching toward another league title against the Dallas Stars, the hit still affected Stevens' state of mind. Meanwhile, Lindros' career was in flux. He wasn't sure if he would ever play again. A feud ensued between the Flyers, Clarke, and the Lindros family. Verbal shots were exchanged in various newspaper stories.

Lindros was scheduled to become a restricted free agent on July 1, 2000. The Flyers made a qualifying offer of $8.5 million U.S. a season, but it was a two-way contract. Lindros considered this a slap in the face and refused the offer. Clarke took it as a trade demand.

Lindros wanted to play for Quinn and his hometown Toronto Maple Leafs. But after a few close calls on a trade between the Maple Leafs and Flyers, a transaction never materialized. The big forward sat out the entire season. He finally was dealt to the New York Rangers on August 20, 2001, 15 months after his last game for Philadelphia and a couple weeks before the Canadian Olympic team's orientation camp in Calgary.

His new home at Madison Square Garden satisfied Lindros. He impressed on a line with Canadian Olympic teammate Theo Fleury and U.S. Olympian Mike York. Lindros played so well he was invited to play in the 2002 NHL All-Star Game as the Rangers representative in Los Angeles. Unfortunately, the injury bug came crawling in his direction once again and he missed the game with a knee ailment.

Lindros wasn't the dominant player he was earlier in his career when in 1994–95 he won the Hart Trophy as the league's Most Valuable Player to his team and the Ted Lindsay Award as the most outstanding player in the entire league as voted by the players. But he still was an elite-level talent who could be a beneficial component of a championship team like the Canadian Olympic squad.

"I don't think I ever played hockey at the same level as I did in Philly and after I got hit by Scott," Lindros said. "But when I got to Calgary [for the orientation camp], I felt pretty good considering I missed a year. I didn't have the strongest season in my first year with the Rangers, but all things considered it was decent.

"I look back to the 2002 team and I'm so grateful to be a part of it. That was a pretty special group and to be included was unforgettable."

Gretzky took a risk to include players like Peca, Fleury, and Lindros on the Canadian roster, especially with the depth of hockey talent in the country. One player who wasn't a risky decision but was absent from the 1998 Canadian Olympic team was Kariya. He was an easy addition to the mix.

This was a guy who loved to represent Canada. He always answered the call from Hockey Canada. Six months before his 20th birthday, Kariya already had played in two world junior tournaments, winning gold in 1993, settled for Olympic silver in that shootout game in 1994, and helped Canada end a 33-year drought with a coveted world championship crown, also in 1994.

He continued his Canadian tour of duty with a second-place showing at the 1996 World Championship. But he was kept out of the 1996 World Cup of Hockey due to a groin injury and suffered a massive setback 18 months later as he readied himself for the 1998 Olympics in Japan. Twelve days before Canada's opener against Belarus in Nagano, Kariya scored in a game against the Chicago Blackhawks and then was cross-checked in the face by opponent Gary Suter, also a U.S. Olympian. Kariya suffered a concussion and didn't return to action until the following season.

His father, T.K., was Japanese Canadian, and Kariya was looking forward to participating in his second Olympic Games in his dad's ancestral homeland.

"It was the biggest disappointment of my career," Kariya said. "To not only miss a chance to represent my country but to miss an opportunity to play in the country of my family's background. It all worked out in the end because I was able to play with a special group and win Olympic gold and be part of the group that won for Canada for the first time in 50 years."

Kariya's concussion was so bad in 1998 he could not even watch the Olympics on television. He suffered from post-concussion symptoms and was confined to a dark room as he recovered. He didn't play again until the following season but regained his form and was a lock to perform for Canada in his second Olympic Games four years later.

Kariya came by his desire to play Canada honestly. Every time he entered the family room in the basement of his home, he would walk by photos of his father in a Canadian jersey playing rugby for the Canadian national team.

"He always said to me that the highest honour you could have as an athlete was to play for your country," Kariya said. "So that was something I always dreamed of doing."

Even though Kariya was one of the best in the game, he was awestruck to show up at the orientation camp in Calgary and find out his roommate was Steve Yzerman. It turns out his sister, Noriko, thought Yzerman was a hockey hunk.

"She was jealous, that's for sure, when I told her who I roomed with," Kariya said. "My sister thought he was the best-looking guy in the world. I thought he was one of the best hockey players in the world. That was unbelievable for me to be staying in the same room, sitting round with him talking about what was going on.

"I learned so much from watching him and some of the other great players on that team, how they prepare for practices and games, how much intensity they had in practices. Martin Brodeur didn't want to let you score in practice."

That intensity was evident in the semifinal against Belarus. Having seven different scorers helped put the Canadian offence on the right track heading into the finale.

"When I'm talking to young athletes, I always tell them the best way to be good tomorrow is to be good today," Kariya said. "We did just that in the Belarus game. I don't remember anyone panicking early on. We needed time, going from the NHL straight to the bigger ice. By the end of the tournament, we collectively felt that nobody was going beat us.

"We just needed time to get our line combinations right and get an understanding of how we needed to play. We just knew we were going to get better and better."

The Lemieux-Kariya-Yzerman line did just that. They had a big game against Belarus and would be significant contributors two days later against the United States.

Sadly for the 27-year-old Kariya, it would be his final game wearing a Canadian sweater, an experience he treasured with three international first-place finishes (2002 Olympics, 1994 World Championship, 1993 World Junior Championship) and two second-place showings (1994 Olympics, 1996 World Championship).

A year after winning gold with Canada in Salt Lake City, Kariya finally advanced to the Stanley Cup Final against Martin Brodeur and the Devils. In Game 6 of the championship series, Kariya was knocked down by New Jersey defenceman Scott Stevens in a hit similar to the one Stevens put on Lindros four postseasons earlier. The difference was that after being attended to in the dressing room, Kariya returned to score a goal and help the Ducks force a seventh and deciding game.

But wouldn't you know it, his old Olympic teammate Brodeur was unbeatable in the final game. He made 24 saves for the shutout in the Devils' 3–0 victory.

Kariya became an unrestricted free agent the next season. He decided to reunite with his old Anaheim teammate Teemu Selanne, who also was an unrestricted free agent after three years in San Jose, on the Colorado Avalanche. But Kariya never hit his stride in Colorado. He was hindered by wrist and ankle ailments and as a result scored only 11 goals in 51 regular season games, his worst season offensively.

Gretzky omitted Kariya from Canada's roster at the 2004 World Cup of Hockey and again for the 2006 Olympics. Gretzky wanted to inject some fresh faces into the lineup for both tournaments and felt Kariya's best play was behind him. Kariya, of course, could not have known that would be the case on the eve of the gold medal final in Salt Lake City.

CHAPTER 8
GOLDEN FINISH

Few people enjoyed the 2002 Winter Games in the manner Bart Hull did. Led by the family's patriarch, Hockey Hall of Famer Bobby Hull, the Hulls usually have been the most jocular in the circles they travelled. Bart was in Salt Lake City to watch his older brother Brett perform for the United States.

Bart realized after the United States' second game he mistakenly had been given a credential that allowed access few enjoyed. As he waited outside a barricade near the United States' dressing room for his brother, five years older, a security guard pointed out he had a coveted pink decal on his credential.

All of a sudden he was a fly on the wall in the U.S. dressing room before games and after games. A fine athlete himself—Bart played fullback in the Canadian Football League with Ottawa and Saskatchewan and was good enough to play several games of minor pro for the Idaho Steelheads of the West Coast Hockey League—this was a neat experience for the younger Hull.

"Herb Brooks was so good to me," Bart Hull said of the U.S. head coach. "I called him Coach, and he told me to call him Herb. The atmosphere in the locker room was incredibly relaxed. They wanted to win after what happened in Nagano, but it was a very loose team."

Besides hanging with his brother and other family members like his mom and brother Bobby Jr., Bart and his full credential enabled him to visit the downtown concert venue to see groups like Train.

About the only event Bart Hull missed was the Tragically Hip concert at the University of Utah on the evening before the gold medal game. Gord Downie, Rob Baker, and the rest of the popular Kingston, Ontario, band entertained Canadian Olympic athletes at what was called the Labatt Blue Olympic Bash.

The Hip opened by sharing the stage with the entire women's hockey team. Many of the women kept the musical beat with tambourines and other assorted improvised percussion instruments. The initial song was "Fireworks," an anthem for all Canadian hockey players because the first few lyrics out of Downie's mouth are: "If there's a goal that everyone remembers, it was back in ol' '72."

This, of course, is in reference to Paul Henderson's late game-winner for Team Canada to clinch the historic Summit Series against the Soviet Union. Downie ended the opening number by saluting the women's team. "Ladies and gentlemen, they've got rhythm." Veteran player Cassie Campbell draped her gold medal around Downie's neck so he could show it off for the rest of the set.

Among the athletes enjoying the atmosphere were Theo Fleury and a handful of the men's players. The start time for the gold medal game would come early the next day, 1 PM local time. Fleury reasoned sleep would be elusive, so he may as well continue to enjoy the Olympic experience.

"The free time can drive you crazy," Fleury said. "The actual playing part is easy. It's the old Malcolm Gladwell thing—10,000 hours of practice. Hockey is a reaction sport. You've put in all this time, so you don't have to think.

"You have very few opportunities to do something like this. To live in the Athletes' Village and get to know other athletes and their stories is part of the experience. It was amazing to be around all these elite Canadian athletes and find out what it took for them to get there."

When Fleury and the Canadians arrived at the E Center for the gold medal game they were met with an electric-charged atmosphere. The Salt Lake City Games began slowly for the Canadian athletes, with the first week mired in the Jamie Sale-David Pelletier controversy. But when that rhubarb settled in the favour of the Canadian pair, the 2002 Olympics turned in Canada's way. Better results emerged.

The path for the men's hockey team was similar. There was a sluggish start that picked up steam, and now Mario Lemieux and his teammates had an opportunity to add a sixth gold medal for Canada to go with three silver and eight bronze for 17 medals, a total that surpassed the country's previous record of 15, set in 1998 in Nagano.

Besides Steve Nash and Bart Hull and a throng of athletes in the 8,599-seat building, there were other VIPs, like the first father of hockey, Walter Gretzky; United States vice president Dick Cheney; former New York City mayor Rudy Giuliani; *Friends* television star Matthew Perry, a Canadian; and Downie, Baker, and the Tragically Hip.

Interestingly, Perry has dual Canadian-U.S. citizenship. He was born in Williamstown, Massachusetts, but raised in Ottawa, Ontario. His mother, Suzanne, was Prime Minister Pierre Trudeau's press secretary.

As a nation nestled in to cheer on Canada, U.S. and Canadian soldiers sat together in the wee hours of the morning in Kandahar, Afghanistan. They needled each other about which country would win bragging rights as a hockey superpower.

Back in the E Center, the buzz already was thick with anticipation. Before the players hit the ice to begin the game, there were competing chants of "U-S-A, U-S-A," and "Can-a-da, Can-a-da." Wayne Gretzky took his seat in the Canadian box. Sitting to the Great One's right was assistant coach Wayne Fleming, who via a headset would be in contact with Ken Hitchcock on the bench. To Gretzky's left were Steve Tambellini, Kevin Lowe, and Bob Nicholson.

The date of the game was not lost on the Canadian players. It was 50 years to the day that Canada had last won gold in the men's hockey tournament. To ease the tension in the dressing room, Canadian head coach Pat Quinn opted for a straightforward message in his pregame discourse. He told his players to go out and play like women, referring to what the Canadian women's team had accomplished three days earlier.

This was a second act of Quinn's game day routine. When he ran into Gretzky, Nicholson, and the management group before the game, Quinn promptly dropped his drawers to show off the lucky briefs and socks his grandchildren had festooned with good-luck glitter.

After Quinn and his assistants went over last-minute instructions, the players nervously paced in the hallway, waiting to take to the ice.

"One of the things I miss about playing the game is that 30 seconds you go from the dressing room to the ice," Fleury said. "There's the energy from the crowd and you have this fresh sheet of paper that you get to write your story on three times a night.

"I remember standing in the hallway before the game and looking out into the arena to see a sea of red and white on one side, red, white, and blue on the other side. You could see all these Canadian and U.S. flags being waved. When I stepped on the ice not only was the hair on the back of my neck standing up, the hair inside my helmet was standing straight up. The anticipation was something else. I remember thinking to myself, 'I need to hit someone right now.'"

Canada wore white to the United States' blue jerseys. Lemieux and U.S. captain Chris Chelios exchanged team pennants, a customary pregame practice in the international game.

Quinn put out the Eric Lindros, Owen Nolan, and Ryan Smyth line to open the intense proceedings. U.S. head coach Herb Brooks countered with his top trio of Mike Modano, John LeClair, and Brett Hull. The Lindros line didn't score any goals, but every time they hopped over the boards they kept the puck in the U.S. zone.

They were, however, on the ice for the game's first goal. It was not because of careless play or a defensive miscue. The U.S. struck first because of a brilliant display of hustle from centre Doug Weight, a teammate of Pronger and MacInnis in St. Louis.

After Canada killed off an early interference penalty to defenceman Scott Niedermayer, United States left wing Tony Amonte kept the puck on a two-on-one rush to beat Canadian goalie Martin Brodeur through his pads. The rush occurred because of Weight's resolve in his own end. A split second before Nolan was going to get to a loose puck in the high slot, Weight dove to poke the puck away from his opponent and out of the U.S. end. Amonte scooped up the result of Weight's determination for the icebreaker.

The U.S. lead only lasted a few shifts. They had another power-play opportunity to increase their lead when Fleury went off for cross-checking. But once again Canada's penalty killing unit was up to the task. Paul Kariya then scored the goal of the tournament thanks to a remarkable play from Lemieux.

This wasn't a dramatic late game-winner like the Tragically Hip sang about Henderson's heroics in 1972 or Darryl Sittler in the 1976 Canada Cup or Gretzky to Lemieux in the 1987 Canada Cup or later

Jarome Iginla to Sidney Crosby at the 2010 Olympics in Vancouver. But this goal was a masterpiece.

The play developed in the neutral zone with Lemieux sliding a pass to defenceman Chris Pronger. He skated along the sideboards and then entered the U.S. zone. Pronger stopped to fire a pass into the slot to a breaking Lemieux. But instead of stopping the puck, Lemieux let it travel through his legs to a hard-charging Kariya. Lemieux's decoy stopped U.S. goalkeeper Mike Richter in his tracks, allowing Kariya to have an open net.

"I'm not sure if he got an assist on that goal," Kariya said. "But it was the greatest assist of a guy who never touched the puck."

Lemieux did register an assist on the tying goal. He fed the puck to Pronger to start the scoring play.

"When the play happened, it was like it was in slow motion," Kariya added. "He had his wrist cocked like he was going to shoot, and this froze Richter. But I knew exactly what [Lemieux] was doing.

"The vision and awareness to do that in a gold medal game was outstanding. I can still see it. There was an understanding there. He didn't have to say a word. I just knew it was coming to me and I had an empty net. We started rolling from there."

Canada did start rolling after Kariya's tying goal. Before the horn sounded to end the first period, Joe Sakic made a brilliant play to set up Jarome Iginla to make it 2–1.

Pronger didn't get an assist on the go-ahead goal, but he made a smart pass to Simon Gagne to start the play up the ice. Gagne found to his left the skilled Sakic, who bought time when he looked back into the high slot as if he was going to slide the puck back to Gagne. In the meantime, Iginla skated hard toward the U.S. goal and fought off defenceman Gary Suter to score at the side of the net on Sakic's hard pass.

Watching Suter get beat on the play no doubt pleased Gretzky and Kariya. Suter, of course, was the bandit who hit Gretzky from behind to knock him out of the 1991 Canada Cup and the same public enemy No. 1 who cross-checked Kariya in an NHL game, forcing him to miss the 1998 Olympics.

The Canadians felt good about the way the first period went. They had the lead. They killed off a couple of penalties. But there were still 40 minutes to play. There was still a long way to travel. Inside the dressing room in the first intermission, Lemieux didn't like the chatter he was hearing. Not one player wanted to be specific, but somebody complained a bit too loudly about a missed call near the end of the period.

"Enough," Lemieux shouted. One word and all was quiet. The focus immediately shifted back to the task at hand.

"I remember that," Smyth said. "I'm getting chills right now thinking about it. You could hear a pin drop. I remember Iginla was sitting beside me and Fleury was on the other side of me. Mario meant business. He wasn't fooling around. You could tell he wanted to win so bad."

This was the first brush with Mario in a high-level tournament for most of the Canadian team. The last time he played for Canada was at the 1987 Canada Cup. He was 22 years old when he converted the famous pass from Gretzky for the championship clincher.

Lemieux was retired when the 1998 Olympics were contested. As he often stated, he was on a beach in Florida when Canada lost the dreaded shootout game against Dominik Hasek and the Czech Republic.

Four years later, the new and improved Canadian group was surprised to discover Lemieux was a down-to-earth superstar. Adam Foote recalled how the dorm area outside the room he shared with

Rob Blake was a gathering place on most nights for the Canadian players. As sure as Pat Quinn would enjoy a late-evening cigar on a bench outside the Olympic Village, another common sight was Lemieux and his 6'4" frame spread out on the couch to give him the best view of the television.

Other Canadian players recalled how positive and friendly the 36-year-old Lemieux was. He always had a smile on his face and often went out of his way to talk to everyone before games. He was a true captain. This portrait was far from the way he was publicly perceived earlier in his career.

"Mario is one of the greatest athletes in any sport," Kariya said. "But he's also a tremendous guy, and a humble guy.

"Anyone of that stature is going to be a leader just by how he performs on the ice. But when you look at that team, we had a lot of quiet leaders. Steve Yzerman became one of the great leaders in the game. He's a quiet guy. I think that's a character trait you see in a lot of the leaders in our sport."

Yzerman was the only one among the 2002 group to have played alongside Lemieux on another Canadian team. But that was way back in 1985 at the world championship in Prague, when Canada dropped a 5–3 decision to the home-country Czechs to settle for silver.

"To have him as a teammate is very reassuring, to know he was on our side," said Yzerman, who also played with Lemieux for the bronze medal Canadian team at the 1983 World Junior Championship. "He was that good or he gave you the feeling that everything would be okay. He'll take charge and he'll get it done.

"In Salt Lake, at that time, he was the best player in the world. He was very sharp, astute, intelligent. But he also was laid back. He sits back and takes it all in."

Yzerman and Lemieux were roommates in 2002. This made for some quiet times, considering Yzerman doesn't say much either. Both prefer to lead on the ice.

"In a tournament like that, the way Mario leads is [when] you need a big goal, he'll score it," Yzerman said. "You need a big play, he'll make it.

"To me, he was like Jean Beliveau. As a little kid I knew a little bit about Jean Beliveau. The way he carried himself with the grace on the ice and with the grace off the ice. That also was my impression of Mario."

The Canadian player who continued to make an impression in the second period was Sakic. Led by the tireless centre, Canada started the middle frame in fine fashion. Richter made an outstanding arm save on Sakic to keep his team close, and a few shifts later Canada hit a post. On a delayed high-sticking call to Hull, Fleury made a dazzling move through the U.S. defence, but lost the puck on his deke.

The Canadians continued to press on the power play. Their efforts resulted in another U.S. infraction. This time, defenceman Aaron Miller got his stick up on Nolan. Canada enjoyed a 5-on-3 advantage, but a third goal proved elusive.

A rebound from a Blake shot went right to Lemieux, but the puck was on edge and his attempt clanked off the post. The game's momentum turned the other way. Canada defenceman Al MacInnis was called for interference after he inadvertently collided with Jeremy Roenick in the Canadian end.

Unlike Canada, the U.S. cashed in on their power-play chance. Brian Rafalski's shot deflected off Pronger's stick and past Brodeur. The game was tied for the second time. But just like in the first period. Canada was quick to score after a U.S. goal. That wonderful Kariya goal arrived six minutes after Amonte's icebreaker. It took Sakic only 2:49 to put Canada back up with a 3–2 lead.

With Roenick in the penalty box for tripping Kariya, Sakic's shot went in off the stick of U.S. defender Brian Leetch. Iginla and Joe Nieuwendyk were in front causing havoc with Richter's power of observation. The Canadians, once again, enjoyed a slim lead as they filed into their dressing room.

As mentioned before, Hitchcock remarked how the Canadian coaches didn't have to do much strategizing once the games started in Salt Lake City because of all the brilliant hockey minds playing. Players like defenceman Rob Blake sounded like a seasoned head coach.

"I've never been more comfortable about a team I coached," Hitchcock said. "I just felt our players were locked in and we didn't have to do much coaching. We said very little between periods. The players were saying to each other the same message we wanted to say.

"At one point in the second intermission, Pat said, 'Listen, we don't have to say anything, they're saying it all.' There was nobody in the world that was going to beat us."

Quinn followed through on his observation. Before he sent out the players for the final 20 minutes, he came out of the coach's office to address them as a group one final time. In his meaty hands he held a bunch of notes. His reading glasses slipped to the end of his nose, as they always did. Before he spoke, he looked around the room. He glanced at Lemieux, then Yzerman, Sakic, Blake, and finally MacInnis.

Quinn crumpled up his notes and deposited his papers in the bin. He then said, "What am I going to tell you guys that you don't already know. Just go out and win the hockey game."

"It was just a brilliant coaching moment by not overcoaching," Canadian forward Michael Peca said.

The U.S., who appeared out of sync with a handful of offsides, played much better in the early stages of the third period. Brodeur was forced to be sharp, turning aside a stuff attempt from U.S. forward Mike York. The game then hit a lull of tight defensive hockey until Yzerman was called for tripping with 6:17 remaining.

There was a close call on the ensuing U.S. power play. But Brodeur made a dandy right pad stop on Hull's blast from the side. Canada survived another penalty. Now it was time to close the deal.

The Sakic line followed up Canada's man-disadvantage situation with another dominant shift. Iginla whistled a wicked shot that was stopped by Richter. However, the puck had enough steam to bound over the U.S. goaltender. Sakic was in perfect position to bat home his second of the game, but he swung and missed. It didn't matter. Iginla's shot slid over the goal line anyway. The dramatic game was now down to its final 3:59. Surely Canada could hang on.

There would be one final goal, a beauty breakaway from Sakic.

"There were nerves and excitement going into the game, but once you settle in, everybody on our team bought in to the short shifts," Sakic said. "It was a game between two teams that badly wanted to win.

"It was so much fun. That was the fastest-paced game I was ever in. Once Iggy scores to make it 4–2 you can breathe a little, but just a little. How many Hall of Famers were there on both teams?"

There were 19 Hockey Hall of Famers—14 on Canada as well as Chelios, Hull, Leetch, Modano, and Phil Housley on the American side.

As good as Sakic was on the ice, he also was a significant part of the veteran Canadian leadership core. His positive attitude was infectious. One of Tambellini's memories of the 10-day Canadian Olympic odyssey was before the Czech game, a day after that quiet ride home from Provo, Utah, for the management group. As Tambellini, Gretzky, Lowe, and Nicholson sipped on their coffees before the Czech game, the chilled Sakic moseyed past the nervous Nellies with some positive words.

"What is wrong with you guys?" Sakic asked. "Don't worry, we're going to win."

Tambellini explained, "It just spoke to why we had such good leadership. They had such a calmness and confidence."

Sakic didn't remember his kind gesture.

"I do remember we were a very confident group," Sakic said. "There were so many veteran guys on that team who had played in so many big games. Obviously, everyone gets ready for big games in different ways, but this group had a quiet and calmness about them and everybody got along so well.

"We came together and trusted each other."

Fittingly, the last goal was scored by Sakic. Gretzky and Yzerman opined that Lemieux was the best player in the world at the time of the Salt Lake City tournament. But the clinic Sakic put forth made a strong case for the Colorado Avalanche captain.

He was named tournament MVP, a performance capped off by his two-goal, four-point finale and a continuation of a remarkable run for him. Sakic played a massive role in the Avalanche's successful Stanley Cup championship run nine months earlier.

He finished second in the NHL scoring race in 2000–01 with a career-high 54 goals for his second-best career point total of 118 points to win the Hart Trophy and Ted Lindsay Award. The latter goes to the league's most outstanding player as determined by his peers.

Sakic also finished second in Selke Trophy voting as the league's top defensive forward in 2000–01. For Canada in 2002, he was a tenacious, two-way performer. He took key faceoffs, killed penalties, played a massive role in man-advantage situations, and centred Canada's most productive line.

When there is a best-on-best tournament like the Canada Cups of the past and then the Olympics, you'll often hear Canadian players state that a key to success is for each player to check their ego at the door. There is no better example of this truism in Salt Lake City than Sakic.

He went from playing alongside Lemieux and Kariya in the opening game to lining up with two of the younger, inexperienced forwards at the time in Iginla and Simon Gagne for the second game.

"I thought, 'Oh man, he's not going to be too excited about that,'" Iginla said. "Really, that's what I thought. We were two of the youngest guys. But right away he came over to us, 'Hey, I'm excited to play with you guys. We're going to have so much fun with all our energy.'

"It just gave Simon and I a huge energy boost. It made us comfortable. He didn't need to do that, but it meant the world to us. He had no attitude. If he was disappointed, he didn't show it.

"Part of finding line chemistry is you want to play with that sort of person, and every mistake isn't a big deal. If you get a feeling a guy doesn't want to play with you, you over-try, especially when that player is a veteran player. You don't want to let him down. Joe got us to relax, to try to play fast and have fun. That made a huge difference for us."

Gagne, a leap year baby in 1980, grew up in Sainte-Foy, a suburb of Quebec City. He was a Nordiques supporter and a big-time Sakic fan, who performed for the Nordiques from 1988 until the summer of 1995 when the franchise relocated to Denver. Gagne couldn't believe his eyes when he entered the Canadian dressing room to find his practice jersey the same colour as Sakic's on the day before the game against Germany.

"I'll never forget it," Gagne said. "He was my hero growing up in Quebec City with the Nordiques. I thought to myself, 'Is this really happening?'

"We were dangerous from the first game on. We just fit, probably because we were each different type of players."

Iginla and Gagne already had bright futures in the game when they arrived in Salt Lake City. But with the benefit of hindsight, the two went on to brilliant careers after playing alongside Sakic and elevating their play.

There was an immediate impact for Iginla. He finished the regular season with 17 goals in his final 24 outings to wind up leading the league with 52 goals. Iginla already had a reputation as a big-situation performer early on, winning back-to-back Memorial Cups with the Kamloops Blazers in 1993–94 and 1994–95 as well as a world junior crown with Canada in 1996. He scored a remarkable 20 goals in 20 postseason outings in 1995.

The world junior stage was enhanced because a few weeks before the tournament, the Calgary Flames traded a beloved Joe Nieuwendyk to the Dallas Stars in exchange for Iginla. With all the increased attention, the teenager didn't miss a beat, leading the tournament with five goals in six games to spark Canada to gold in Boston in 1996. How appropriate he won Olympic gold for the first time with Nieuwendyk as a teammate.

After the 2002 Olympics, Iginla's next biggest stage arrived when he scored 13 goals in 26 playoff games to help the underdog Flames advance all the way to a seventh and deciding game in the 2003–04 Stanley Cup Final against the Tampa Bay Lightning.

A league championship eluded Iginla, but not Gagne. Two years after playing so well for the Flyers in their losing bid in the 2009–10 Final against the Chicago Blackhawks, Gagne signed with the Los

Angeles Kings. Even though he couldn't contribute as much as desired due to a serious neck injury, he earned a championship ring with the Kings.

Gagne was 21 and in his third NHL season when he arrived for the Winter Games. He would go on to score 47 goals in 2005–06 and followed up that impressive season with a 41-goal year.

"That was a breakout year for Jarome," Sakic said, discussing the success of the line in Salt Lake City. "After Game 1, Pat [Quinn] put me with Jarome and Simon, two of the younger guys, and I enjoyed playing with them.

"To see them elevate their games was special. We obviously had a lot of veterans on the team. But we couldn't have done it without the young guys on the team."

After Sakic's final goal, the Canadians in the crowd began to serenade their heroes with "O Canada" in the dying seconds of the historic 5–2 victory. Thousands back home streamed onto the streets to celebrate on the 17th day of the Salt Lake City Olympics. Canada had extended its record medal count to 17.

The men's hockey team successfully followed up what the women accomplished three days earlier, pushing Canada into rarified air of a triumph that had never happened before—a double gold in hockey. Finally, Gretzky, Lemieux, and Co. had ended 50 years of frustration for a hockey nation.

"It was just an incredible experience," Fleury said. "When you grow up playing road hockey in Russell, Manitoba, and it's minus-50, you dream about playing in the Stanley Cup Final, not playing in the Olympic gold final."

Maybe Quinn remembered the Edmonton Mercurys and their Olympic gold in 1952. He was nine at the time. But none of the players were born back then. The oldest player, MacInnis, was born

11 years after the Mercurys' victory. The youngest, Gagne, came to life a whopping 28 years after 1952. As one of the dozen members from the Canadian team in Nagano—and oldest—MacInnis was appreciative to get a second chance and be part of the group that ended the five-decade drought.

"At age 38, to hear that anthem is unbelievable," he told reporters after the game. "After Nagano, I was depressed for two weeks. I didn't know if I'd get another shot.

"I can't imagine what they're doing in Canada right now. Well, actually, I know what they're doing. They're having a cold one on us and it's well deserved."

To watch the different pockets of celebrations and conversations on the ice after Canada clinched its championship was compelling. After the group hug, high up in the stands, between Gretzky, Lowe, Tambellini, and Nicholson, and their wives, Gretzky made his way to the Canadian bench with his wife, Janet. One of the first embraces the Gretzkys engaged in was with Lemieux.

"If you look at the National Hockey League over the years, guys like Mark Messier, Bobby Orr, or Jean Beliveau, the bigger the game the better they performed," Gretzky said. "Mario gave us a big-time performance in 2002.

"And he gave us an effort on and off the ice. Enough can't be said about what he did for us as a leader. When you walk into a dressing room and you have the likes of Mario sitting there, and Al MacInnis, Pronger, Curtis Joseph, and Marty Brodeur, you followed them and fit in."

Lemieux was beaming. His comeback from cancer and his hip problems were capped off by another magical moment. Nobody was condemning him now for playing through pain and his decision not to opt out so a younger Joe Thornton could take his place.

"This is awesome," Lemieux said after the treasured victory. "Three and a half years ago I was sitting on a beach in Florida, so to have a chance to come back and play with these great players is very special.

"All we've talked about since August is winning the gold. I brought my three daughters, my son, and my whole family down for this because it was the chance of a lifetime. When you're born there, you're always going to be Canadian."

As Gretzky shared a moment with Quinn, Lemieux skated over to the U.S. bench to salute Brooks. Back in 2002, Brooks' day job was as a pro scout for Lemieux and the Penguins.

"Let's just say I didn't ask for a raise," Brooks replied, when asked what he and Lemieux chatted about. "We exchanged greetings. He came over to shake hands. He's a great guy."

After his masterful coaching job in the U.S. Miracle on Ice in 1980, Brooks received a shot in the NHL with the New York Rangers, Minnesota North Stars, and New Jersey Devils. But he never captured the Olympic magic in the pro game, failing to advance past the second round of the playoffs in any of his seven seasons behind an NHL bench. He began working in the scouting department of the Penguins in 1995. The organization allowed Brooks time off from his duties in 1998 to coach France at the Olympics, but France finished 11th in Nagano.

His final coaching stint in the NHL was with the Penguins, a year before Lemieux decided to un-retire. Brooks replaced Kevin Constantine after 25 games in the fall of 1999 and steered them into the playoffs, but Pittsburgh was eliminated in a six-game loss to Gagne and the Philadelphia Flyers in the second round.

Sadly, like Quinn and Fleming, Brooks did not make it to the 20th anniversary of the 2002 gold medal game. Six days after his 66th birthday on August 11, 2003, he was driving along Interstate 35, about a half-hour north of the twin cities of Minneapolis-St. Paul, Minnesota. He died as the result of a single-car accident. Reports indicated Brooks fell asleep at the wheel. He wasn't wearing a seat belt. A year later, Disney released its inspiring movie *Miracle*, starring Kurt Russell as Brooks.

"You were born to be hockey players, every one of you, and you were meant to be here tonight," is the way part of Brooks' impassioned speech before the game against Russia was portrayed in the movie. "This is your time. Their time is done. It's over. I'm sick and tired of hearing about what a great hockey team the Soviets have. Screw 'em. This is your time. Now go out there and take it!"

Bart Hull remembered Brooks' speech before the 2002 gold medal final was subdued. Bart told Brooks, "That was a little different than last time."

To which Brooks replied, "This is different. These guys are pros, and what am I going to tell them? Your brother makes $9 million a year."

Jeremy Roenick and his U.S. teammates were hoping to make it their time 2.0. But the Canadians were too invincible on this late February afternoon.

"This is huge for Canada," a classy Roenick said after the game. "A huge monkey is lifted off Canada's back. Both teams deserved to be here, and they got big goals today. It was a great game. Today was their day.

"There are a lot of people singing and dancing in Canada. This is what they've waited for, for a long time. I'm happy for them."

Another classy move from the losing side came from Modano. He met up with his old coach Hitchcock, who had been fired by the Dallas Stars less than a month before Salt Lake City. Modano gave Hitchcock a congratulatory bear hug.

Over in another corner were three Detroit Red Wings team-mates, Yzerman and his U.S. counterparts, Chelios and Hull. There was a victory party for Yzerman to attend and emotional wounds to heal for Hull and Chelios. But in a couple of days the three would reunite, along with Shanahan, and come together to try to win another Stanley Cup in Motown.

On the Canadian side, many of the players peered into the stands, searching for parents, family, and friends. Taking a cue from Canadian star Hayley Wickenheiser, who carried her stepson Noah onto the ice for the gold medal celebrations on Thursday, Nieuwendyk and Peca each did the same.

Tyra Nieuwendyk was a newborn when she was lifted over the glass and into her dad's arms.

"It was because of Gretz," Nieuwendyk recalled. "We were standing around the ice in front of the bench. I could see my wife and my brother behind the bench, right behind the glass partition. I was waving toward them in the emotion of the moment.

"[Gretzky] said, 'Get your brother to hand her down.' It was something else to have her in my arms at that time."

The memories of that celebration come flooding back for Nieuwendyk and Peca whenever they see a photo of their children with them amid the postgame frolics.

"My son [Trevor] was 16-17 months old," Peca remembered. "He was sick for two weeks leading up to the Olympics. My wife, Kristin, was holding him the whole game. If there was a time she needed a break, it was then. It was so cool to have him on the ice. The photo I love is my son looking at the medal after it was put around my neck."

IIHF president Rene Fasel presided over the medal ceremony as each Canadian player received his golden prize. Fleury was the first to receive his medal from Fasel. As Fasel made his way down the line, near the end you could see a thoughtful Scott Niedermayer quietly coast to the final spot. He didn't want the team's third goalie, Ed Belfour, who had joined his teammates on the ice in his sweater but wearing black dress pants, to be the last one to receive his gold medal.

One of the Canadian players, Owen Nolan, was doing his best impression of renowned documentarian Ken Burns and filming as much of the celebration as possible.

After a late-game shift with his linemates, Nolan left the bench with about two minutes still on the game clock to retrieve his small hand-held camera from the dressing room.

"I had thought about this before the game," Nolan confessed. "I had a pretty good feeling that we were going to win. I wanted something to remember the experience, something to show my family and friends."

And what if Quinn called his line for one final time?

"I guess I would have told him I was too busy," Nolan said, laughing. "You know the saying, 'Words can't describe something like this?' Well, I felt it was better to have a tape of it."

When Fasel made his way to Nolan, Yzerman did his teammate a solid and filmed Nolan's medal presentation. For his part, Nolan shared the video with his friends and family a few times, but now the keepsake is stored away.

Before the Canadian players left the ice, there was one more tradition to take care of—the team photo at centre ice. This was a custom that had been started by Gretzky, Lowe, and the Oilers in 1988 after they won their fourth Stanley Cup championship in five years. The Oilers had become the first team in league history to win 11 home playoff games that spring. So after they defeated the Boston Bruins in the series finale, following their victory lap, they gathered at centre ice with the Stanley Cup to pose for the team photo.

If you look at the photo from 2002, you can't miss the big Irish coach in the back, standing with his left arm around his daughter, Kalli. Before Quinn started shaking hands and hugging trainers, assistant coaches, and players, he locked eyes with Canadian security man Keith Hammond. The latter was a former Vancouver cop who did some security detail with the Canucks when Quinn was in charge of the NHL team.

Quinn asked Hammond before the game to lasso his wife, Sandra, as well as daughters Kalli and Val, and bring them down to the bench if Canada was victorious. The head coach wanted to make sure Hammond didn't forget. So Hammond hurried up to the concourse, found the Quinns, and swiftly brought them down to ice level.

"He raced us down past all the Olympic security on the event level and right to the bench," Kalli said. "Dad grabbed my hand and said, 'Come on, you're in the picture.' I said no, but he had a good hold on my hand and said, 'Yes, you are, so come with me or we'll miss it.'"

Her father was so proud of his group when the Canadian national anthem was played.

"Every time I hear the national anthem it takes me right back to being on the ice with him," Kalli said. "It doesn't matter if it's a sporting event or something else that the anthem is played—it's something I always have."

To her ears, and memory, a proverbial solid gold hit.

As the Canadian players filed into the dressing room in euphoria, they were quick to settle down and enjoy a job well done. Gretzky took a congratulatory phone call from Canadian Prime Minister Jean Chretien.

The players chatted with each other as they sipped on Bud Lights, recalling moments in the game and in the tournament. They talked about the sluggish start and how the team continued to improve the more time they spent together.

"The team needed time," Shanahan said. "The start galvanized us. It gave us an us-against-the-world mentality. It didn't turn around for us right away, but it was a start. We had belief.

"I'll never forget what Kevin Lowe said to me in the dressing room about an hour after the game. He said the only disappointment for him was he wanted to see how good this team would be in a week."

Lowe felt this team hadn't reached its peak in the gold medal final, in which Canada outshot the U.S. 39–33 and held its opponents to only nine shots on goal in the final period.

"The final was a masterpiece," Lowe explained. "It was classic domination. I'm not saying that at times earlier the game wasn't teetering. Brett Hull had that chance in the third period and there were other times the game could have gone either way. But overall, they didn't have a ton of chances. I thought we were in complete control."

CHAPTER 9

Two Decades Later

There were two visitors to the Canadian dressing room as the victory party rocked on. The first was NHL commissioner Gary Bettman, who presented Joe Sakic with his tournament MVP award. The second chap was pacing out in the hallway, patiently waiting to be summoned inside the hockey sanctuary.

His name was Trent Evans, an ice maker from Edmonton, Alberta, who played a unique role on the periphery of Canada's win. Evans was lured for a month-long stay in Salt Lake City to make sure the E Center had an ice surface worthy of the game's best.

This was the NHL's idea. If its players were competing, the league wanted to make sure quality ice was in place to properly showcase the talent. The league hired Dan Craig away from Edmonton to help improve ice conditions around the NHL in 1997. The Northlands Coliseum, home to the Edmonton Oilers' five championships, was renowned for having the best ice. That's where Craig earned his ice-guru reputation, and that's where Evans continued the building's fast-ice tradition.

Craig was told to make sure the ice for the 2002 Olympics was top-notch. So he enlisted the services of Evans to whip the E Center's surface into shape. On the second day there, he noticed there was no centre ice faceoff dot. He inquired if he should paint one on. The answer was yes, but not the foot-long diameter dot employed in the

NHL. Craig instead told Evans he wanted a dot about the size of a loonie, a Canadian dollar coin.

The request gave Evans an idea. Why not position a loonie just below the ice surface at centre ice as a good-luck charm for the Canadian men's and women's teams? Evans, however, did not have a Canadian dollar coin on him that day, so he embedded a bluenose Canadian dime beneath the surface to mark where the loonie-sized faceoff dot was to be located. He returned the next day to plant a 1987 loonie on top on top of the dime, just below the surface.

He told Duncan Murray, also from Edmonton, his roommate and co-worker in Salt Lake City, about the manoeuvre. For the most part, what became known as the Lucky Loonie stayed a secret. Canadian assistant general manager Kevin Lowe found out about it and shared the tale with Wayne Gretzky.

Somehow, the Canadian women's team knew about the loonie, too.

So when Hayley Wickenheiser and her teammates defeated the United States in the gold medal final, a few of the Canadian players went to dig up the loonie. Gretzky observed this from the Canadian bench. He, along with Lowe and Hockey Canada czar Bob Nicholson, had made their way down to ice level after the emotional win.

Gretzky frantically told Nicholson to stop the women from digging up the good-luck charm. Mission accomplished. The loonie remained in its new home for another three days.

"It was pretty incredible to be there," Evans said. "I was there working, so I didn't get the same vibe as say the Canadians who were down there to cheer on the athletes and teams. But I still got pretty nervous watching the women's and men's games."

After Joe Sakic and the men's team finished off the United States, Evans found his way to the Canadian bench. He watched the hand-shake procession, the medal presentation, the victory lap, and the team photo. The plan was for Lowe, his wife, Karen, and Evans to dig out the Lucky Loonie. Evans wanted Lowe to present the coin to Gretzky.

But Lowe had a better plan. He wanted Evans himself to hand it to the Great One. So Evans bided his time in the bowels of the E Center, waiting for Lowe to wave him into the dressing room. Gretzky asked for quiet, to relay the Lucky Loonie story with Evans by his side. Gretzky then announced the Lucky Loonie was going to the Hockey Hall of Fame.

"It was pretty cool of Kevin not to take the limelight and let me give it to Wayne," Evans said. "You know, when kids ask me about it, I tell them the players won the game. I just happened to do something pretty cool."

The loonie did indeed find a place in the Hockey Hall of Fame in Toronto. The dime? Well, Evans still has it in his possession, safe and sound in his security deposit box.

There was another visit to the Canadian dressing room that gold medal day that Gretzky will never forget. As part of his pregame routine, Gretzky would stop by the dressing room, grab a coffee, chat with the players, and wish them well.

On the day of the gold medal final, what caught Gretzky's eye was a prone Steve Yzerman on the trainer's table. His troublesome stiff and swollen right knee was being worked on by athletic therapist Ken Lowe, the older brother of Kevin Lowe. Gretzky, Yzerman, and Lowe exchanged pleasantries. No. 99 departed from the dressing room in search of another distraction before the big game when he was chased down in the hallway by Ken Lowe.

"I just want you to know how bad Steve's knee is," Lowe told Gretzky. "If this was the seventh game of the Stanley Cup Final, I probably would advise him not to play."

Gretzky replied, "Well then, thank goodness this is the Olympic gold medal final.

"Steve basically played on one knee that day and I'll always remember that because he showed the passion the players had for wanting to play for Canada and wanting to win.

"It's one thing to play and play hurt. But it's another thing to play hurt and play so well. That's the one thing that impressed me so much. That's how good these guys were. That's how hard they worked and that's how much they wanted to win."

For his part, Yzerman downplayed the severity of his injury when asked about it two decades later. But the ferocity of the pain the Detroit Red Wings captain endured in order to suit up for Canada became apparent a few days later. He returned to Detroit and did not play another game for six weeks.

"Honestly, I knew I had a sore knee, but I didn't exactly know what was wrong," Yzerman confessed. "I had surgery prior to the Olympics, played in two games [for Detroit] and I felt pretty good. It felt normal.

"Halfway through the first period in the first game against Sweden I thought, 'This is a struggle.' My knee started to swell up and started to get sore. I didn't know what was wrong. But I made a commitment. I told Wayne I was ready to go.

"You either play or you don't play."

His Canadian teammates knew Yzerman played hurt in Salt Lake City. They saw him and others like Lemieux spend plenty of time in the trainers' room undergoing therapy. They just didn't know Yzerman was, as Gretzky stated, performing on one leg.

When Yzerman returned to Detroit he was examined by the Red Wings medical staff and prescribed rest. He was in the middle of his 19th of 22 NHL seasons. He had already suited up for more than

1,350 regular season outings, more than 150 Stanley Cup playoff games, and played 57 times for Canada in a world junior, a Canada Cup, three world championships, a World Cup, and two Olympics.

His knees simply had endured too much wear and tear over time.

"When you get older you develop a lot of aches and pains," said Yzerman, who first injured his knee 14 years previously. "My knees were wearing out. The plan was to rest and rehab."

The Red Wings announced two days after the gold medal game that their captain would miss the next two and a half weeks. His injury was described as a flare-up. It was revealed that he was to receive two injections a week apart and be back in action in short order.

This was on Tuesday, February 26, 2002. He didn't play again until April 10, returning for the Red Wings' third to last game of the regular season. Yzerman took the final two games off but dressed for each of Detroit's 23 playoff games. Remarkably, he finished second in the playoff scoring race with six goals and 23 points, four behind leader Peter Forsberg of the Colorado Avalanche.

Yzerman would win the third and final Stanley Cup of his career. The Red Wings dispatched Canadian teammate Ed Jovanovski and the Vancouver Canucks in six games in the first round; Al MacInnis, Chris Pronger, and the St. Louis Blues in five games in the second round; Rob Blake, Adam Foote, Joe Sakic, and the Avalanche in the West final in a heated seven-game series; and the Carolina Hurricanes in five games in the championship.

When Brendan Shanahan scored twice, including the title-clincher, in Detroit's 3–1 victory in Game 5 against Carolina, Shanahan and Yzerman became the second and third players in hockey history to win Olympic gold and then the Stanley Cup a few months later. Ken Morrow, U.S. Olympian and later New York Islanders defence-man, was the first to turn the trick in 1980.

"2002 was one of the best years of my life," Shanahan said. "Olympics, Stanley Cup, and my twins [Maggie and Jack] were born in November."

Shanahan also became a U.S. citizen in May 2002. While he was riding high, Yzerman considered options on what to do with his ruined right knee. He decided to undergo realignment surgery at the University of Western Ontario in London, performed by Dr. Peter Fowler on August 2, 2002. It was Yzerman's third knee operation in two years.

The latest procedure was rare for hockey players. It called for Fowler to saw the right tibia in the lower leg about halfway down. The surgeon then inserted a donor bone to realign the leg. About a week later, Yzerman remarked there were no guarantees the surgery would allow him to play without pain. He also stated he would retire if there was too much discomfort when he could skate again.

Yzerman was expected to be out of the Red Wings lineup until February. He didn't play again until February 24, 2003. He didn't score until his 10th game that winter. Detroit was swept 4–0 in the first round of the playoffs that spring by Paul Kariya and the Anaheim Ducks.

Besides Yzerman's predicament, it was interesting to see the immediate fallout the days after the Canadian gold medal victory in Salt Lake City. In the first night of action, two days later, Michael Peca scored twice in his New York Islanders 3–3 draw against the Boston Bruins. New York Rangers Eric Lindros and Theo Fleury would beat their Canadian teammate Martin Brodeur for a goal apiece, but Scott Niedermayer would score, too, in the New Jersey Devils' 4–3 win. Brodeur made 21 saves. U.S. goalie Mike Richter of the Rangers took the night off in favour of backup Dan Blackburn.

Simon Gagne checked in with a goal and an assist in his Philadelphia Flyers' 5–4 win at home versus the Chicago Blackhawks. Shanahan, still playing with a fractured right thumb from the Olympics, scored twice, including the game-winner, in Detroit's 4–3 victory against the Tampa Bay Lightning.

Pronger and Jovanovski each had two assists in the Blues' 4–4 tie in Vancouver. Blake set up Sakic and Sakic assisted on another in the Avalanche's 2–2 tie at home against Jarome Iginla and the Calgary Flames.

In his first game back in Toronto, goalie Curtis Joseph fractured his catching hand and would miss six weeks. The next evening, Mario Lemieux picked up two assists in a 5–4 loss to the Los Angeles Kings to become the seventh player in NHL history to reach the 1,600-career-point milestone. But the points would be the last in the Magnificent One's season.

Before the game, Lemieux admitted to experiencing pain in his right hip. He also revealed the pain almost prohibited him from finishing his Olympic experience. But he was given a painkiller shot and had his hip heavily wrapped in order to play.

"I had one chance to play in the Olympics, and I took advantage of it," Lemieux told Pittsburgh reporters after arriving home from Salt Lake City.

A day after the game against the Kings, however, the Penguins announced Lemieux would sit out the remainder of the season to rehab his hip ailment. Tests revealed chronic tendinitis in one of Lemieux's hip flexor muscles as well as an inflamed hip capsule.

It didn't take long for the newly minted gold medalists to return to normal life. In fact, imagine you're Iginla. One moment you're on the receiving end of a Sakic pass to score the most significant goal in your life, the next day you're on a private plane bound for Denver

with Blake, Foote, and Sakic, all of whom will be your opponents in
the first game back.

"Any of these international tournaments you're fortunate enough
to be part of, there is so much to learn from," Blake said. "Whether it's
coaches or great players, you pick up on certain things.

"You win the gold medal and you get an appreciation of the guys
you didn't know that well and a new appreciation for some of the
guys you knew better. I remember flying home with Joe and Adam
and Jarome and we have to play each other again. Of course, Jarome is
playing just as hard as he did in the gold medal final. It took one shift
back in Colorado to see his approach to the game."

While Iginla, Niedermayer, Pronger, and Brodeur reunited for
golden success in 2010 at the Vancouver Olympics, the last hurrah
for most of this bunch together was two and a half years after the
2002 victory at the 2004 World Cup of Hockey, played in Montreal
and Toronto. Eric Brewer, Brodeur, Foote, Gagne, Iginla, Jovanovski,
Lemieux, Niedermayer, Sakic, and Smyth played significant roles for
the winning side. Goalie Ed Belfour (back), Blake (shoulder), Pronger
(foot), and Yzerman (eye) were selected for the team but couldn't play
due to injuries.

The Canadian management team and coaching staff were
the same, with Gretzky, Kevin Lowe, Steve Tambellini, and Bob
Nicholson joining forces with coaches Pat Quinn, Wayne Fleming,
Ken Hitchcock, and Jacques Martin.

This time, the tournament evolved somewhat stress-free for
Canadians. They handled the United States 2–1, Slovakia 5–1, and
Russia 3–1 in the preliminary round and continued their unbeaten
ways with a 5–0 win against Slovakia in the quarterfinals, 4–3 in overtime against the Czechs, and 3–2 against Finland in the final.

This Canadian team was led by the 2002 Olympians. Brodeur was in goal for five of the six victories and put forth a .961 save percentage. He was named to the tournament All-Star team with Foote. Sakic scored the game-winner in the first game against the U.S. Smyth scored twice in the preliminary-round victory against Slovakia. Lemieux set up Sakic to put Canada ahead 3–0 early in the third period of the Russian game.

In the quarterfinal shutout win against the Slovaks, Iginla scored twice and added an assist. Sakic checked in with a goal and two assists. Brewer and Lemieux registered two assists apiece. Brewer and Lemieux put Canada ahead 2–0 in the semifinal against the Czech Republic. Smyth set up Vinny Lecavalier for the overtime winner.

In the final, Lemieux and Brewer combined for Sakic's game-opening goal. Niedermayer put Canada ahead 2–1 and Smyth helped set up Shane Doan's tournament-clinching goal. The final would be the last meaningful game for Lemieux.

A lockout would knock out the entire 2004–05 NHL season. Lemieux returned for the following season to play with the Penguins' No. 1 overall selection in the 2005 NHL draft, Sidney Crosby. But his season would last only 26 games.

There was thought Lemieux would perform for Canada one final time at the 2006 Olympics in Turin, Italy. Gretzky and Quinn would again be running the team and they craved veteran leadership. But even though Lemieux was a point-a-game producer through his first 20, he withdrew his name from consideration on Saturday, December 10, 2005, 11 days before the Canadian roster was to be announced.

Yzerman already had bowed out, citing his play was not up to his standards. Lemieux had a heart episode earlier in the week of Yzerman's pronouncement and was diagnosed with an irregular heartbeat.

"I enjoyed playing in the 2002 Olympics, especially winning the gold," Lemieux said in a statement to announce he wouldn't play for Canada four years later. "It was a great experience, and I would've loved to be there this year. But considering my play so far, the way I've been feeling, and some of the young guys we have for Team Canada, I think it's much better to go that route."

Nobody wore No. 66 on the Canadian team in 2006. In a tribute to Yzerman, the same was the case for his No. 19, even though Sakic, Shane Doan, Brad Richards, and Joe Thornton each sported the number with their respective club teams.

Lemieux would play his final game on December 16, 2005, a 4–3 overtime loss to the Buffalo Sabres. He and Crosby would assist on Ziggy Palffy's late-game goal to send the affair into extra time. His heart condition, diagnosed as atrial fibrillation, forced Lemieux into retirement for good on Tuesday, January 24, 2006.

"This is it, and it hurts," Lemieux said at his retirement press conference. "If I could play this game at a decent level, I'd come back and play. This is really a new NHL, and it's built on speed and young guys.

"I don't want to take pills the rest of my life. It's not something I want to go through. I don't feel great when I wake up. Even to this day I am not feeling 100 per cent, and it's frustrating to me."

He was 40 and retreated to life as the Penguins owner—a Stanley Cup owner, as it turned out. He watched Crosby steer Pittsburgh to titles in 2008–09 as well as back-to-back crowns in 2015–16 and 2016–17.

From the 2002 Canadian Olympic team, Theo Fleury was the first to play his last game in the NHL, on April 4, 2003. He went through a mess of a final season with Chicago. He was involved in a barroom brawl in Columbus; placed on waivers, where no team claimed him;

and finally suspended indefinitely after the season for violation of the substance abuse program.

He played the 2005–06 season for the Belfast Giants in Northern Ireland, and helped them with the Elite Ice Hockey League regular season title. He also played some senior hockey. Still bothered by the way his NHL career concluded, Fleury attempted a comeback at the Calgary Flames training camp in 2009. It was a wonderful story. He scored a shootout winner and checked in with a goal in his final of four exhibition games. But he ended his bid to play again on September 28, 2009, retiring for good.

Al MacInnis was the first from the 2002 Canadian team to officially retire. He played three games at the beginning of the 2003–04 season but was forced to the sidelines because of an eye injury. In 2001 a high stick from San Jose Sharks defender Scott Hannan nicked MacInnis' left eye. He chose to wear a corrective contact lens rather than undergo surgery at the time. He was warned that his eyes could weaken as a result.

That occurred early in October 2003. There was no bodycheck, no high stick, or errant puck. His vision was off after a game. He underwent a three-hour operation to repair a detached retina in his left eye and tighten the retina in his right eye. He was three months past his 40th birthday but held out hope he would return. After all, he finished second in the Norris Trophy voting in 2002–03.

MacInnis took until Friday, September 9, 2005, to announce his retirement. He had healed from his eye problems, but because of the lockout-cancelled 2004–05 season, he was away from the game too long to properly mount a comeback. He made a seamless transition into the St. Louis Blues front office and had his name etched on the Stanley Cup for a second time in 2019, 30 years after winning the prized trophy with the 1988–89 Calgary Flames.

MacInnis' decision to step away from the game was the beginning of a sad week for the NHL. Scott Stevens, Ron Francis, Mark Messier, James Patrick, and Vincent Damphousse each made up their minds before training camps opened to end their careers after the year-long lockout.

After MacInnis and Lemieux ended their superior careers, Yzerman was the next of the 2002 Canadian team to pack it in. He rebounded nicely from his realignment knee surgery to play full seasons before and after the lockout. But he knew, after 22 campaigns and many injuries, his time was up. Even in his last playoff run in 2006, he suffered through a painful rib injury.

His final game was a 4-3 loss in Edmonton against the Oilers. Yzerman's Red Wings were eliminated in six games. Extending best wishes in the handshake line after the outing were his 2002 Canadian teammates Peca, Pronger, and Smyth. Yzerman served as the Red Wings captain for 19 of his 22 seasons, an NHL record.

After Yzerman called it a career, the game slowly waved goodbye to the playing days of the 2002 Canadian Olympic team over the next 11 years. Next to retire were Eric Lindros and Joe Nieuwendyk in 2007, followed by Belfour (2008), Joseph (2009), Peca (2009), Shanahan (2009), Sakic (2009), Fleury (2009), Blake (2010), Kariya (2010), Niedermayer (2010), Foote (2011), Owen Nolan (2011), Pronger (2012), Jovanovski (2014), Smyth (2014), Brodeur (2014), Brewer (2015), and Gagne (2015).

Iginla was the final member of the 2002 Canadian Olympic team to play in the NHL on April 9, 2017, while with the Kings. He assisted on a goal from Dustin Brown midway through the third period to give Los Angeles a 3–2 lead. But the Kings lost to the Anaheim Ducks 4–3 in overtime.

There were whispers Iginla would play for Canada at the 2018 Olympics in Pyeongchang, South Korea, when commissioner Gary Bettman refused to allow the participation of NHL players to continue in the Winter Games. But Iginla knew his time was up. Quietly, his final game was the end of an era for the 2002 golden men on the ice.

In the end, the 23 played a combined 26,710 regular season games in the NHL as well as another 2,416 in the Stanley Cup playoffs. Belfour, Brodeur, and Joseph combined for 1,629 regular season wins and 356 more in the postseason.

Imagine the trophy case for this group. Belfour (two) and Brodeur (four) combined to win six Vezina Trophy honours and nine more Jennings Trophies for the lowest goals against average. Brodeur won five of these awards to Belfour's four.

There were four Calder Trophy Rookie of the Year winners in Belfour, Brodeur, Lemieux, and Nieuwendyk. Blake (1998), MacInnis (1999), Niedermayer (2004), and Pronger (2000) each won a Norris Trophy as the NHL's defenceman of the year. Pronger also won the Hart Trophy as MVP in 2000 to join other MVP winners Lemieux (1988, 1993, 1996), Lindros (1995), and Sakic (2001). Lindsay Award winners, the most outstanding player as voted by the players, were garnered by Iginla (2002), Lemieux (1986, 1988, 1993, 1996), Lindros (1995), Sakic (2001), and Yzerman (1989).

Art Ross Trophy scoring titles were claimed by Lemieux (1988, 1989, 1992, 1993, 1996, 1997) and Iginla (2002). Iginla also won a pair of Rocket Richard trophies as the top goal scorer in 2002 and 2004. Peca (1997, 2002) and Yzerman (2000) were Selke Trophy winners as the best defensive forward. Kariya (1996, 1997) and Sakic (2001) claimed the Lady Byng Trophy as the most gentlemanly player.

Conn Smythe winners as the playoff MVP also were aplenty with MacInnis (1989), Lemieux (1991, 1992), Sakic (1996), Yzerman (1998), Nieuwendyk (1999), and Niedermayer (2007).

After Blake, Sakic, and Shanahan became members of the Triple Gold club in 2002 as winners of Olympic gold, world championship crown, and Stanley Cup, Niedermayer joined the elite group with a world championship win in 2004. Pronger skated into the club when he won the Stanley Cup in 2007 with Anaheim.

How many Stanley Cups among this group? There were a whopping 27, led by Niedermayer's four (1995, 2000, 2003, 2007). There were three apiece from Brodeur (1995, 2000, 2003), Nieuwendyk (1989, 1999, 2003), Shanahan (1997, 1998, 2002), and Yzerman (1997, 1998, 2002); two apiece from Lemieux (1991, 1992), Foote (1996, 1997), and Sakic (1996, 2001); as well as one each from Belfour (1999), Blake (2001), Fleury (1989), MacInnis (1989), and Pronger (2007).

Iginla became the 14th member of the group to become inducted into the Hockey Hall of Fame in 2020. He was preceded by Brodeur (2018), Kariya (2017), Lindros (2016), Pronger (2015), Blake (2014), Niedermayer (2013), Shanahan (2013), Sakic (2012), Belfour (2011), Nieuwendyk (2011), Yzerman (2009), MacInnis (2007), and, of course, Lemieux (1997). There could be more additions. Cases could be made for Fleury, Foote, and Joseph.

Meanwhile, in 2020, Kevin Lowe was inducted into the Hockey Hall of Fame, joining his old Oilers teammate, Gretzky (1999). Pat Quinn was included in the builders' category posthumously in 2016. Ken Hitchcock and Bob Nicholson likely will one day hear their names called, too.

In 2012, at the World Junior Championship in Calgary, Hockey Canada invited members from past Canadian teams to celebrate the success of its junior program of excellence. It just so happened that Russ Courtnall and Pat Quinn were there. Courtnall had captained the 1984 team. Quinn coached Canada to gold in 2009 in Ottawa.

There was a dinner party scheduled at the downtown Keg one evening when Hockey Canada president Bob Nicholson had an idea.

"Hey Pat, I never did tell you the story about how you got the job for 2002, did I?" Nicholson told Quinn. "Come meet the guy who got you the job."

Nicholson then relayed the story about how Courtnall vouched for Quinn to Gretzky after their round of golf that summer day in 2000. Quinn didn't know what to say, so he smiled at Courtnall, shook his hand, and bought him a glass of wine.

"He put out his big paw and said, 'Let me shake your hand,'" Courtnall recalled.

So many from the 2002 group stayed in the pro game and several remain involved. Lemieux still owns the Penguins. Brodeur is part of the Devils' front office. He was also an assistant general manager to Sean Burke in building the bronze medal-winning 2018 Canadian Olympic team.

Nieuwendyk moved into the Dallas Stars GM's office from 2009 to '13. Foote coached major junior with the Kelowna Rockets. Joseph was a goalie consultant with the Carolina Hurricanes. Pronger enjoyed a spell in the league's department of player safety as well as a stint as assistant GM with the Florida Panthers.

Blake, Shanahan, Sakic, and Yzerman have enjoyed long stints in management. Shanahan initially made the transition of player to NHL vice president of hockey and business development in 2009 and moved into the senior vice president's role as chief disciplinarian two years later. In April 2014, Shanahan was placed in charge of his hometown Toronto Maple Leafs as club president.

Shanahan hired Blake to work in the NHL hockey operations department in 2010 and he stayed in that role until he was lured back to the Kings prior to the 2013–14 season to become the club's assistant GM. He also helped Hockey Canada as GM of the 2014 World Championship team and was elevated to the Kings' GM in 2017. Sakic moved into the Avalanche's front office in 2011 in an advisory position. He expanded his portfolio to become the team's executive vice president of hockey operations two years later.

"We loved playing the game and we wanted to stay part of it," Sakic said. "You don't want to let go. You love the competition, and you want to stay a part of the fraternity."

While Blake won a Stanley Cup as an executive in his first year back with the Kings, Sakic has built the Avalanche into a contender, advancing all the way to the West final in 2019–20.

The 2002 Olympic graduate with the most success as an executive has been Yzerman. He took over the Tampa Bay Lightning in 2010 and swiftly built the Sunshine State team into a contender. The Lightning advanced to the 2014–15 Stanley Cup Final against the Chicago Blackhawks. Yzerman was named the winner of the Jim Gregory General Manager of the Year Award that season. The Lightning won the Stanley Cup five years later, but Yzerman had returned to his beloved Red Wings to replace longtime GM Ken Holland on April 19, 2019.

It's interesting to see all the different paths the players took after 2002 and some of the proverbial reunions. For example, Shanahan and Brodeur were teammates in New Jersey in Shanahan's final season in 2008–09. As Oilers GM Lowe brought in Pronger and Peca, and with Smyth already in Edmonton, the Oilers advanced to the 2005–06 Stanley Cup Final, only to lose in seven games to the Carolina Hurricanes.

"That's one of the great things about being involved with teams like this for international tournaments," Lowe said. "You get to peek behind the curtain of certain players and get to know them better as a player and a person."

Smyth later became teammates with Sakic in Colorado. Pronger and Niedermayer found themselves together in Anaheim and won the 2006–07 Stanley Cup. Pronger then moved on to Philadelphia, where he became a teammate of Gagne and went to a third final in five years.

One of Yzerman's first moves as Lightning GM was to trade for Gagne, a few weeks after the 2009–10 championship series. Yzerman also acquired Brewer from the St. Louis Blues at the 2011 trade deadline. Iginla was a popular former teammate from 2002. Sakic signed him as a free agent in 2014 and traded Iginla to Blake and the Kings in 2017.

"We had a little insight on the type of player he was," Blake said with a chuckle.

Quinn also got in on the act. He brought to Toronto Nieuwendyk, Lindros, Nolan, and Belfour after the 2002 Olympics.

"He was a great man," Nolan said of Quinn. "I was happy to reunite with him in Toronto."

Belfour and Nieuwendyk finished their NHL careers with the Florida Panthers, playing for head coach Jacques Martin.

Meanwhile, Ken Hitchcock coached Gagne in Philadelphia and Peca with the Columbus Blue Jackets. In his role as coach and managing partner with the Arizona Coyotes, Gretzky signed unrestricted free agents Jovanovski and Nolan in 2006.

Gretzky had one final fling as the Canadian executive director after the 2002 Olympic success and the repeat performance at the 2004 World Cup of Hockey. He returned for the 2006 Olympics in

Turin, Italy, two months after losing his mother, Phyllis, to lung cancer. He brought back with him the same management team of Lowe and Tambellini and coaching staff of Quinn, Fleming, Hitchcock, and Martin.

Although Yzerman and Lemieux withdrew their names from consideration, there were some familiar faces from 2002 in Brodeur, Blake, Foote, Pronger, Gagne, Iginla, Sakic (as team captain), and Smyth. Gretzky boasted the 2006 edition was deeper than 2002, but the magic couldn't be re-created.

The team not only was a disaster, but there was also too much outside noise surrounding it. A week before the 2006 Olympics, Gretzky's assistant coach with the Coyotes, Rick Tocchet, was charged in a New Jersey–based illegal gambling ring and Gretzky's wife, Janet, although never charged, was implicated as a frequent partner.

Todd Bertuzzi was also embroiled in controversy. As the tournament began, former Avalanche forward Steve Moore filed a civil suit in Ontario court, seeking $19.5 million in damages for an on-ice incident that ended Moore's career and involved Bertuzzi in March 2004. The sides reached a confidential out-of-court settlement in October 2014.

Scott Niedermayer couldn't play in 2006, opting instead to undergo arthroscopic right knee surgery over the Olympic break.

Gretzky received heavy criticism for not including Penguins rookie Sidney Crosby on the roster. But this was a team that was never in sync. Martin Gerber made 49 saves for Switzerland to blank Canada 2–0 in its third of five preliminary-round games. Finland's Antero Niittymaki followed suit with a 30-save 2–0 shutout against Canada the next day.

Canada rebounded to win in its preliminary-round finale. Richards, Martin St. Louis, and Pronger scored first-period goals for a three-goal lead and hung on for a 3–2 victory against the Czech Republic. But in the quarterfinals against Russia, the Canadians were blanked 2–0.

The horrible performance from Canada wasn't quite as embarrassing as Belarus over Sweden (the Tre Kroner, by the way, won gold in Turin), but this was the worst performance from Canada in a men's Olympic tournament since a sixth-place showing in Lake Placid, New York, in 1980. In Italy, Canada scored only three goals in its final four games and was blanked in 11 of the final 12 periods.

After Turin, Gretzky told Nicholson he had enough. It was time to find a successor. Gretzky helped Nicholson compile a shortlist of replacements. But just as Clarke advocated for Gretzky for 2002, Gretzky had in mind his heir apparent, urging Nicholson to go hard after Yzerman.

Nicholson contacted Yzerman that summer to gauge his interest. The Cranbrook, British Columbia–born talent, who was raised in Nepean, Ontario, wanted to be involved. But before the details were ironed out, Yzerman accepted an invitation to be the general manager of the Canadian teams for the 2007 and 2008 World Championships in Moscow, Russia, and Quebec City, Quebec, respectively.

For Moscow, Yzerman was assisted by a familiar face in Martin as well as John Ferguson Jr., then GM in Toronto. Brewer was the team's assistant captain. The tournament went as smoothly as possible with Canada defeating Finland 4–2 in the gold medal final. Canada went a perfect 9–0. Canada settled for silver after a 5–4 loss to Russia in the 2008 final.

Now came the matter of the 2010 Canadian Olympic team. But before he jumped into the pressure-filled position, Yzerman asked Nicholson to set up a meeting between him, Nicholson, and Gretzky.

"Steve didn't want to take over the executive director role, as it was known, unless he got Wayne's blessing," Nicholson said. "By that he meant he wanted to talk to him. I told Wayne that and he said, 'He doesn't need that.'"

So Nicholson was caught in the middle. He had to come up with a plan to facilitate a meeting between the two. Nicholson found his opening. The city of Brampton, Ontario, was going to open a new facility and name it after retired Canadian women's team star Cassie Campbell. The date for the ceremony to christen the Cassie Campbell Community Centre was Saturday, September 13, 2008.

Nicholson invited both Yzerman and Gretzky to attend the festivities and both accepted.

"We get to this thing and there were 350, 400 people there," Nicholson recalled. "We were there together at the beginning, but then got separated. I then see Wayne and he tells me that he has to get out of there.

"I said, 'Wayne, we've got to get Stevie and meet with him.' So I went over and found Steve. We found a corner and the three of us talked. It wasn't a long conversation, but it was a powerful one."

Gretzky was upfront. He confessed it was no picnic being in charge of the Canadian Olympic team. He outlined the pressure and the headaches and the time Yzerman would need to commit. Gretzky also applauded Yzerman's hockey IQ, just like Clarke praised No. 99 for his smarts a decade earlier.

"He told Steve that he was the right person for the job because of his personality and what he had been through in his career," Nicholson said. "Just to hear Wayne's words and to see how appreciative Stevie was, it was something special to listen to."

Yzerman accepted the job on the spot. The three of them kept the transaction quiet. Gretzky, however, two days after the Brampton gathering, revealed he would not be the Canadian Olympic team executive director for Vancouver in 2010. In an interview with The Fan 590's *Hockey Central*, a radio program in Toronto, he cited he would be too busy with his coaching duties for the Coyotes. Gretzky, however, did volunteer he was open to helping out the 2010 Canadian team in any other capacity.

When Hockey Canada officially swore in Yzerman as Gretzky's replacement on October, 18, 2008, Gretzky was named an advisor. Yzerman kept Lowe on the management team and added Ken Holland as well as then St. Louis assistant GM Doug Armstrong.

Yzerman stated he wouldn't name a coach until the end of the 2008–09 NHL season. The job would not go to Gretzky. No. 99 took himself out of the running at the same time Yzerman was named the Canadian executive director. Mike Babcock was appointed Canadian head coach in June 2009. His assistants were Hitchcock, Jacques Lemaire, and Lindy Ruff.

"We had these team dinners in Salt Lake, the night before games," Yzerman said. "I'd be sitting there beside Shanny and we'd be nervous about the next game. We'd look at one end of the table and there would be Wayne, Bob, Kevin, and Steve enjoying a glass of wine, looking nice and relaxed.

"I said to Shanny, 'That's going to be us one day. It looks like a lot more fun than this [playing].' But then to be in their shoes, it was incredibly fun and exciting, but stressful.

"Canada is always the favourite, always expected to win. All you can really do is screw it up. It's a great experience, but all you can do is hold your breath and hope it works out."

It did work out for Yzerman. Canada won in 2010, and again four years later in Sochi, Russia, as Yzerman stayed on for one final Olympics. In Sochi, Canada won all six starts and outscored the opposition 17–3 in what Yzerman described as Canada's best defensive performance.

But was the 2002 team the best ever, Olympics, Canada Cup, or World Cup? Yzerman was noncommittal, saying all the teams were great from Bobby Orr's last hurrah at the 1976 Canada Cup to Gretzky and Lemieux in 1987 to 2002 to 2014.

Most of Yzerman's teammates from 2002 agreed that to crown the best Canadian team was too difficult to bestow because each situation was different.

"By the end of the tournament we collectively felt that nobody could beat us," Kariya said. "We just needed time to get our line combinations right and get an understanding of how we needed to play. We just knew we were going to get better and better."

"We always had an excuse in the Olympics because our best weren't there," Niedermayer added. "The excuses were no longer there when NHL players started to participate. It didn't quite work out in 1998.

"This was a pivotal moment in Canadian hockey. It was time to get the job done and bring the men's [Olympic] gold back home."

Canada's 2002 gold medal performance wasn't the first successful dance for the men's hockey team. It wasn't the last dance, either. But it likely was the most important dance.

"These guys were so good," Gretzky said. "They worked so hard. They wanted to win so badly. I can't say enough good things about being a part of it.

"It was the thrill of a lifetime."

ACKNOWLEDGMENTS

Twenty years ago, I was the assistant sports editor at Canada's national newspaper, the *Globe and Mail*. I was more comfortable reporting than leading back then. But for the 2002 Winter Olympics, I was blessed working alongside six splendid journalists in covering 17 days of events that would captivate most of Canada.

Stephen Brunt, James Christie, Eric Duhatschek, Fred Lum, Allan Maki, David Shoalts, and Beverley Smith were a dream team.

On February 3, 2002, I arrived in Salt Lake City five days before the opening ceremony for the Winter Olympics. It was Super Bowl Sunday. Maki and I discovered the Dead Goat Saloon, a superb joint in downtown Salt Lake City, to take in Tom Brady's first NFL title with the New England Patriots.

Three weeks later, Mario Lemieux and the Canadian men's Olympic hockey team capped off the Winter Games with a gold medal effort in the concluding competition. The celebration back home transformed into quite the party.

The men's hockey gold ended a five-decade-long Olympic drought for Canada, and the triumph should be saluted. There was 1972 and Gretzky to Lemieux in 1987. In 2002, there was no Sidney Crosby golden goal, like in 2010. But there was a massive amount of resiliency with this Canadian team. This was a calm and confident group, and by the end, a dominant bunch.

The inside story needed to be told. So thanks to Wayne Gretzky, Bobby Clarke, and Bob Nicholson, and the management group, the coaching staff, and the 23 players for sharing their recollections. Of course, we all miss the late Pat Quinn. But his thoughtful daughter, Kalli, was in Salt Lake City for the championship journey, and she was so helpful in telling his side of the story.

Thanks to editor Michelle Bruton and the Triumph team for making this idea a reality, and to literary agent Brian Wood for believing in this project and persuading Triumph to get behind it.

Fred Lum has my gratitude for his vivid photographs. Thanks to *Globe and Mail* publisher Phillip Crawley for allowing Fred's work to be part of this book.

Thanks to the late Christie Blatchford, Kevin Carroll, Don Douglas, Bob Elliott, Perry Lefko, Scott Morrison, and Franklin Zicarelli for their friendship, counsel, and encouragement.

Finally, I'm forever indebted to the wonderful Kathy Broderick for putting up with me, not just with this project, but for decades in the past and hopefully in the future.

APPENDIX

Box Scores of Canada Men's Hockey at 2002 Olympic Games

Sweden 5–2 Canada [February 15, 2002] 16:10 UT
E Center, West Valley City

FIRST PERIOD

1. Canada—Blake (Peca, Fleury) 2:37
2. Sweden—Sundin (Alfredsson) 5:30

Penalties—Sundin SWE (holding) 11:31

SECOND PERIOD

3. Sweden—Sundstrom (Nylander, Naslund) 6:06
4. Sweden—Sundin (Alfredsson, Lidstrom) 10:42
5. Sweden—K. Jonsson (Zetterberg) 11:47
6. Sweden—Dahlen (Sundstrom, Sundin) 15:58 (pp)

Penalties—MacInnis CAN (high-sticking) 15:18

THIRD PERIOD

7. Canada—Brewer (Nolan) 15:39

Penalties—Olausson SWE (delay of game) 0:27, Ragnarsson SWE (tripping) 7:16

SHOTS ON GOAL BY

Sweden 10 11 4–25

Canada 15 3 17–35

Goal—Sweden: Tommy Salo; Canada: Curtis Joseph

Power-plays—Sweden 1/1; Canada 0/3

Referee—Dennis LaRue (USA); Linesmen—Sergei Kulakov (RUS), Dan Schachte (USA)

Attendance—8,597

Canada 3-2 Germany [February 17, 2002] 19:00 UT
Peaks Ice Arena, Provo

FIRST PERIOD

No scoring

Penalties—Lindros CAN (roughing) 0:24, Ehrhoff GER (cross-checking)
7:59, Pronger CAN (high-sticking) 13:00

SECOND PERIOD

1. Canada—Sakic (Gagne) 8:59

2. Canada—Kariya (Nolan) 14:23 (pp)

3. Canada—Foote (Jovanovski, Nieuwendyk) 18:25

Penalties—Blake CAN (tripping) 4:35, Kunce GER (roughing major, game
misconduct) 13:24

THIRD PERIOD

4. Germany—Lott (MacKay, Ludemann) 7:36

5. Germany—Hecht (Schubert, Abstreiter) 13:51 (pp)

Penalties—Lindros CAN (high-sticking) 3:19, MacInnis CAN (tripping)
12:16

SHOTS ON GOAL BY

Germany 8 4 8–20

Canada 10 17 10–37

Goal—Germany: Marc Seliger; Canada: Martin Brodeur

Power-plays—Germany: 1/5; Canada: 1/3

Referee—Bill McCreary (CAN); Linesmen—Johan Norrman (SWE), Tim
Nowak (USA)

Attendance—6,425

Canada 3–3 Czech Republic (February 18, 2002) 16:10 UT
E Center, West Valley City

FIRST PERIOD

1. Canada—Lemieux (Niedermayer) 9:11
2. Czech Republic—Havlat (Jagr) 18:23

Penalties—MacInnis CAN (hooking) 6:12, Dopita CZE (hooking) 15:29, Foote CAN (slashing) 19:51

SECOND PERIOD

3. Czech Republic—Havlat (Kubina) 3:08
4. Canada—Lemieux (Yzerman) 18:49

Penalties—Kaberle CZE (holding) 5:22, Rucinsky CZE (hooking) 12:23.

THIRD PERIOD

5. Czech Republic—Dopita (Hamrlik) 13:17
6. Canada—Nieuwendyk (Fleury, Jovanovski) 16:36

Penalties—None

SHOTS ON GOAL BY

Czech Republic 6 7 16–29

Canada 13 15 8–36

Goal—Czech Republic: Dominik Hasek; Canada: Martin Brodeur

Power-plays—Czech Republic: 0/2; Canada: 0/3

Referee—Bill McCreary (CAN); Linesmen—Dan Schachte (USA), Sergei Kulakov (RUS)

Attendance—8,599

Canada 2–1 Finland [February 20, 2002] 20:15 UT
E Center, West Valley City

FIRST PERIOD

1. Canada—Sakic (Gagne) 3:00

Penalties—None

SECOND PERIOD

2. Canada—Yzerman (Lemieux) 15:49

3. Finland—Hagman (Kallio, Jokinen) 16:09

Penalty—Selanne FIN (interference) 5:52

THIRD PERIOD

No scoring

Penalty—Jovanovski CAN (boarding) 6:10

SHOTS ON GOAL BY

Finland 5 8 6–19

Canada 15 14 5–34

Goal—Finland: Jani Hurme; Canada: Martin Brodeur

Power-plays—Finland: 0/1; Canada: 0/1

Referee—Dennis LaRue (USA); Linesmen—Mike Cvik (CAN), Rudolf
    Lauff (SVK)

Attendance—8,599

Canada 7–1 Belarus (February 22, 2002) 12:00 UT
E Center, West Valley City (Semifinal)

FIRST PERIOD

1. Canada—Yzerman (Sakic, Blake) 6:05
2. Belarus—Salei 13:24
3. Canada—Brewer (Yzerman) 17:25

Penalties—Kopat BEL (high-sticking) 1:52, Mikulchik BEL, Fleury CAN
   (roughing) 16:05

SECOND PERIOD

4. Canada—Niedermayer (Lemieux, Kariya) 2:09 (pp)
5. Canada—Kariya (Yzerman, Lemieux) 13:28

Penalties—Kovalev BEL (holding) 1:10, Jovanovski CAN (tripping) 2:38,
   Peca CAN (cross-checking) 5:11, Mikulchik BEL (boarding) 9:59

THIRD PERIOD

6. Canada—Gagne (Peca) 5:21 (sh)
7. Canada—Lindros (Smyth, Nolan) 12:24 (pp)
8. Canada—Iginla (Shanahan) 16:15

Penalties—Niedermayer CAN (high-sticking) 3:31, Fleury CAN
   (hooking) 6:56, Nolan CAN (roughing) 8:43, Belarus bench (too many
   men; served by Makritsky) 10:52, Tsyplakov BEL (roughing), Lindros
   CAN (slashing) 17:43, Tsyplakov BEL, Lindros CAN (unsportmanlike
   conduct) 19:54

SHOTS ON GOAL BY

Belarus 3 6 5–14
Canada 17 15 19–51
Goal—Belarus: Andrei Mezin (27–23), Sergei Shabanov (24–21); Canada:
   Martin Brodeur
Power-plays—Belarus: 0/5; Canada: 2/3
Referee—Stephen Walkom (CAN); Linesmen—Sergei Kulakov (RUS),
   Tim Nowak (USA)
Attendance—8,599

Canada 5-2 United States [February 24, 2002] 13:00 UT
E Center, West Valley City [Gold Medal Final]

FIRST PERIOD

1. United States—Amonte (Weight, Poti) 8:49
2. Canada—Kariya (Pronger, Lemieux) 14:50
3. Canada—Iginla (Sakic, Gagne) 18:33

Penalties—Niedermayer CAN (interference) 3:04, Fleury CAN (cross-checking) 10:03

SECOND PERIOD

4. United States—Rafalski (Modano) 15:30 (pp)
5. Canada—Sakic (Jovanovski, Blake) 18:19 (pp)

Penalties—Hull USA (hooking) 9:27, Miller USA (high-sticking) 10:19, MacInnis CAN (interference) 14:40, Roenick USA (tripping) 16:30

THIRD PERIOD

6. Canada—Iginla (Yzerman, Sakic) 16:01
7. Canada—Sakic (Iginla) 18:40

Penalties—Yzerman CAN (tripping) 13:43

SHOTS ON GOAL BY

United States 10 14 9–33
Canada 11 17 11–39
Goal—United States: Mike Richter; Canada: Martin Brodeur
Referee—Bill McCreary (CAN)
Power-plays—United States: 1/4; Canada: 1/3
Referee—Bill McCreary (CAN); Linesmen—Mike Cvik (CAN), Antti Hamalainen (FIN)
Attendance—8,599

Table A: Final Standings

Finish	Country	Wins	Losses	Ties	Goals For	Goals Against	Points	
1	Canada	4	1	1	22	14	9	* Gold
2	United States	4	1	1	26	10	9	* Silver
3	Russia	3	2	1	19	14	7	* Bronze
4	Belarus	3	6	0	18	42	6	
5	Czech Republic	1	2	1	12	8	3	
5	Finland	2	2	0	12	10	4	
5	Germany	3	4	0	15	26	6	
5	Sweden	3	1	0	17	8	6	
9	Latvia	2	1	1	20	14	5	
10	Ukraine	2	2	0	11	14	4	
11	Switzerland	2	1	1	11	10	5	
12	Austria	1	3	0	8	13	2	
13	Slovakia	1	2	1	15	13	3	
14	France	0	3	1	7	17	1	

Table B: Results

1	2002-09-02	Group A	Germany	3-0	Slovakia
2	2002-09-02	Group A	Latvia	4-2	Austria
3	2002-09-02	Group B	Belarus	1-0	Ukraine
4	2002-09-02	Group B	France	3-3	Switzerland
5	2002-10-02	Group A	Germany	3-2	Austria
6	2002-10-02	Group A	Latvia	6-6	Slovakia
7	2002-11-02	Group B	Ukraine	5-2	Switzerland
8	2002-11-02	Group B	Belarus	3-1	France
9	2002-12-02	Group A	Austria	3-2	Slovakia

10	2002-12-02	Group A	Germany	4-1	Latvia
11	2002-13-02	Group B	Switzerland	2-1	Belarus
12	2002-13-02	Group B	Ukraine	4-2	France
13	2002-14-02	Final Qualifying	Latvia	9-2	Ukraine
14	2002-14-02	Final Qualifying	Switzerland	4-1	Austria
15	2002-14-02	Final Qualifying	Slovakia	7-1	France
16	2002-15-02	Group C	Sweden	5-2	Canada
17	2002-15-02	Group C	Czech Republic	8-2	Germany
18	2002-15-02	Group D	Russia	6-4	Belarus
19	2002-15-02	Group D	United States	6-0	Finland
20	2002-16-02	Group D	Finland	8-1	Belarus
21	2002-16-02	Group D	Russia	2-2	United States
22	2002-17-02	Group C	Sweden	2-1	Czech Republic
23	2002-17-02	Group C	Canada	3-3	Germany
24	2002-18-02	Group C	Canada	3-3	Czech Republic
25	2002-18-02	Group C	Sweden	7-1	Germany
26	2002-18-02	Group D	United States	8-1	Belarus
27	2002-18-02	Group D	Finland	3-1	Russia
28	2002-20-02	Quarterfinals	Belarus	4-3	Sweden
29	2002-20-02	Quarterfinals	Russia	1-0	Czech Republic
30	2002-20-02	Quarterfinals	United States	5-0	Germany
31	2002-20-02	Quarterfinals	Canada	2-2	Finland
32	2002-22-02	Semifinals	Canada	7-1	Belarus
33	2002-22-02	Semifinals	United States	3-2	Russia
34	2002-23-02	Bronze Medal	Russia	7-2	Belarus
35	2002-24-02	Gold Medal	Canada	5-2	United States

Table C: Leading Scorers

		Games	Goals	Assists	Points	+/-	PIM
SWE	Mats Sundin	4	5	4	9	4	10
USA	Brett Hull	6	3	5	8	4	6
USA	John LeClair	6	6	1	7	2	2
CAN	Joe Sakic	6	4	3	7	6	0
SVK	Marian Hossa	2	4	2	6	5	0
SUI	JJ Aeschlimann	4	3	3	6	0	2
FRA	Philippe Bozon	4	3	3	6	1	2
GER	Len Soccio	7	3	3	6	3	8
CAN	Mario Lemieux	4	2	4	6	4	0
CAN	Steve Yzerman	6	2	4	6	4	2

Table D: Leading Goalies

		Minutes Played	Goals Against	Goals Against Avg.	Save %	Shutouts
SUI	Martin Gerber	157.44	4	1.52	0.96	0
USA	Mike Richter	240	9	2.25	0.932	1
RUS	Nik Khabibulin	359.12	14	2.34	0.93	1
SWE	Tommy Salo	179.03	7	2.35	0.924	0
CZE	Dominik Hasek	239	6	2.01	0.924	0

Table E: Tournament All-Star Team

G	Mike Richter	USA
D	Brian Leetch	USA
D	Chris Chelios	USA
F	John LeClair	USA
F	Joe Sakic	CAN
F	Mats Sundin	SWE
	MVP	Sakic
	BEST GOALIE	Khabibulin
	BEST D-MAN	Chelios
	BEST FORWARD	Sakic

Table F: Canadian Roster

No.	Player	Height	Weight	Age	Birth Date	G	A	Points	+/-	GWG
4	Rob Blake	6'4"	225	32	Dec. 10, 1969	1	2	3	2	0
3	Eric Brewer	6'3"	220	22	April 17, 1979	2	0	2	0	1
74	Theo Fleury	5'6"	181	33	June 29, 1968	0	2	2	1	0
52	Adam Foote	6'2"	214	30	July 10, 1971	1	0	1	1	1
21	Simon Gagne	6'0"	185	21	Feb. 29, 1980	1	3	4	5	0
12	Jarome Iginla	6'1"	209	24	July 1, 1977	3	1	4	4	0
55	Ed Jovanovski	6'2"	212	25	June 26, 1976	0	3	3	1	0
9	Paul Kariya	5'10"	172	27	Oct. 16, 1974	3	1	4	5	0
66	Mario Lemieux	6'4"	225	36	Oct. 5, 1965	2	4	6	4	0
88	Eric Lindros	6'4"	236	28	Feb. 28, 1973	1	0	1	-3	0
2	Al MacInnis	6'2"	209	38	July 11, 1963	0	0	0	3	0
27	Scott Niedermayer	6'1"	201	28	Aug. 31, 1973	1	1	2	5	0
25	Joe Nieuwendyk	6'1"	205	35	Sept. 10, 1966	1	1	2	0	0
11	Owen Nolan	6'1"	212	29	Feb. 12, 1972	0	3	3	-2	0
37	Michael Peca	6'0"	190	27	March 26, 1974	0	2	2	0	0
44	Chris Pronger	6'6"	220	27	Oct. 10, 1974	0	1	1	2	0
91	Joe Sakic	5'11"	194	32	July 7, 1969	4	3	7	6	1
14	Brendan Shanahan	6'3"	220	33	Jan. 23, 1969	0	1	1	-1	0
94	Ryan Smyth	6'1"	190	25	Feb. 21, 1976	0	1	1	-4	0
19	Steve Yzerman	5'11"	185	36	May 9, 1965	2	4	6	4	1

No.	Goalies	Height	Weight	Age	Birth Date	Minutes	Goals Against	GAA	Save %
20	Ed Belfour	5'11"	194	37	April 21, 1965	0	0	0	0
30	Martin Brodeur	6'2"	205	29	May 6, 1972	300	9	1.8	0.917
31	Curtis Joseph	5'11"	190	32	April 29, 1969	60	5	5	0.8